Que® Quick Reference Series

Norton Utilities®
Quick Reference

George Sheldon

Que® Corporation
Carmel, Indiana

Norton Utilities Quick Reference.

Library of Congress Catalog Number: 89-063562

ISBN 0-88022-508-4

92   91   90   4 3

Interpretation of the printing code: the rightmost double-digit number is the year of the book's printing; the rightmost single-digit number is the number of the book's printing. For example, a printing code of 89-4 shows that the fourth printing of the book occurred in 1989.

This book is based on The Norton Utilities: Advanced Edition Version 4.5 and The Norton Commander Version 2.0.

Que Quick Reference Series

The *Que Quick Reference Series* is a portable resource of essential microcomputer knowledge. Whether you are a new or experienced user, you can rely on the high-quality information contained in these convenient guides.

Drawing on the experience of many of Que's best-selling authors, the *Que Quick Reference Series* helps you easily access important program information.

Now it's easy to look up often-used commands and functions for 1-2-3, dBASE IV, WordPerfect 5, Microsoft Word 5, and MS-DOS, as well as programming information for C, Turbo Pascal, and QuickBASIC 4.

Use the *Que Quick Reference Series* as a compact alternative to confusing and complicated traditional documentation.

The *Que Quick Reference Series* also includes these titles:

1-2-3 Quick Reference
1-2-3 Release 2.2 Quick Reference
1-2-3 Release 3 Quick Reference
Assembly Language Quick Reference
AutoCAD Quick Reference
C Quick Reference
dBASE IV Quick Reference
DOS and BIOS Functions Quick Reference
Hard Disk Quick Reference
Harvard Graphics Quick Reference
MS-DOS Quick Reference
Microsoft Word 5 Quick Reference
PC Tools Quick Reference
QuickBASIC Quick Reference
Turbo Pascal Quick Reference
WordPerfect Quick Reference

Publishing Director
    Lloyd J. Short

Product Director
    Karen A. Bluestein

Editors
    Shelley O'Hara
    Cheryl Robinson

Technical Editor
    Ron Holmes

Indexer
    Sharon Hilgenberg

Production
    David Kline
    Lori A. Lyons
    Jennifer Matthews

Table of Contents

Introduction

Norton Utilities Quick Reference includes the quick reference information you need to work with Norton Utilities, Norton Utilities Advanced Edition, and The Norton Commander. This book includes the most frequently used information you need to manage your computer's disk drives and to perform the commands that make operating your computer easier.

Norton Utilities Quick Reference is divided into two parts. The first part covers Norton Utilities and Norton Utilities Advanced Edition commands; the second part covers The Norton Commander.

Each part provides an alphabetical list of commands. Suppose, for example, that you need to know the total size of all the files located within a certain directory so that you can copy those files to another disk. The information you need is located under the "File Size" section. This section, as well as the others in the book, contains the information you need to understand and execute the command.

This book reviews the various commands, options, and applications available in The Norton Utilities. Because it is a quick reference, this book is not intended to take the place of the extensive documentation included with The Norton Utilities. For example, the documentation includes a thorough discussion on how to determine what is wrong and how to repair a damaged disk. This Quick Reference does not repeat that extensive documentation. Rather, this book tells you how to start the commands that may fix your disk.

Now you can put essential information at your fingertips with *Norton Utilities Quick Reference*—and the entire Que Quick Reference series.

Hints for Using This Book

As you read this book, keep the following conventions in mind:

When Norton Utilities commands are specified in this guide, the command that you must type appears in **boldface blue** type. For example,

From the DOS prompt, type **DT A: /D** and press **Enter**.

To choose this command, type the boldfaced keys, **DT**, press the space bar, type **A:**, press the space bar, type **/D**, and then press **Enter**.

To follow a procedure instructing you to choose an item from a menu, such as

Select **D**isk Information

use the cursor-movement keys to highlight the selection, and press **Enter**, or simply type the boldface letter, in this case **D**.

Information that you see on-screen appears in a `digital` typeface.

The Norton Commander offers mouse support, but you cannot use a mouse in The Norton Utilities Advanced Edition and The Norton Utilities Standard Edition. Although you do not need a mouse to use The Norton Commander, using a mouse makes operating the program easier.

THE NORTON UTILITIES

The Norton Utilities enables you to take charge of your computer and your files. The following sections introduce and explain those commands contained in The Norton Utilities.

Throughout this section, the program you must run to use the particular menu option is directly listed under each header.

For example, the header "Cursor Size" is followed by "NCC". To use the Cursor Size command, therefore, you must be in the Norton Control Center.

Batch Enhancer

BE

Purpose

Creates dynamic batch files by using The Norton Utilities batch file enhancement programs, such as ASK, BEEP, or SCREEN ATTRIBUTES. These subcommands are listed under BE (Batch Enhancer) subcommands. For instance, to find more information on ASK, see BE ASK.

Syntax

BE *subcommand*

   or

BE *filespec*

You can substitute one of The Norton Utilities Batch file enhancement programs for *subcommand*. The batch file enhancement programs include ASK, BEEP, BOX, PRINTCHAR, ROWCOL, WINDOW, and SA.

Notes

Execution of the various Norton Utilities follows the standard rules of DOS in that you can execute in one of two ways:

- From the DOS prompt (C:>)
- Integrated into batch files

Although you can execute the Batch Enhancer
Subcommands from the DOS prompt, they serve a more
useful purpose when integrated into your batch files.

Note: Always include the proper path to Norton Utilities
in your AUTOEXEC.BAT file. This ensures that Norton
will start from anywhere within your disk drive.

BE Ask

BE ASK

Purpose

Prompts you for a response to a specific question. By
using ASK, you can create interactive batch files that
allow conditional branching or decision making based
on your response. The ASK command provides an easy
way to create extensive batch files that execute different
commands, depending on what you input at the time you
run the batch file.

Syntax

BE ASK *prompt* [,*keys*] [DEFAULT=*key*]
[TIMEOUT=*n*] [ADJUST=*n*][*color*]

prompt	A text string that is displayed when the command runs. The prompt usually explains each choice in the key-list. If you include spaces or commas, you must enclose the entire text string in quotation marks.
keys	An optional list of keys, such as characters, symbols, or numbers, one of which you type as a response.

DEFAULT=*key*   Entered within the timeout
                 period. If you press **Enter**, the
                 batch program returns this key.

TIMEOUT=*n*   The time, in seconds, before the
                 default key is returned. If *n* is
                 equal to zero, or if no
                 TIMEOUT is specified, ASK
                 waits forever.

ADJUST=*n*   Adjusts the return value by this
                 amount. Adjust allows
                 multilayered menus to be tested
                 in one pass.

color   An optional color specification
                 for the text of the display
                 prompt.

Notes

As the ASK command runs, it displays the prompt text
and then awaits a response. To make effective use of the
ASK command, your prompt should usually list the keys
you can type in response to the ASK command (any of
the keys in the key-list) and explain the results of
choosing each. You answer ASK by typing any one of
the keys in the key-list. The key-list is not displayed on-
screen; only the prompt you created is displayed. The
key-list is an optional feature of ASK. IF no key-list is
used, any key you press is accepted.

When you choose one of the keys in the key-list (or any
key, if no key-list is specified), ASK returns control of
the computer to the batch file. ASK always passes the
key you selected as an ERRORLEVEL code. The first
choice (the key you can select) in the key-list
corresponds to ERRORLEVEL 1, the second to
ERRORLEVEL 2, the third to 3, and so on. If no key-
list is supplied, ASK always returns ERRORLEVEL 0
in response to any key you press. The batch program
then branches to the different labels in the batch file, in
accordance with the preset ERRORLEVEL codes
contained in the batch file.

Because of the way batch file ERRORLEVEL codes work, always list the IF ERRORLEVEL *n* GOTO LABEL statements in descending order of ERRORLEVELs. For example, you must list ERRORLEVEL codes like this:

```
IF ERRORLEVEL 5, GOTO ...
IF ERRORLEVEL 4, GOTO ...
IF ERRORLEVEL 3, GOTO ...
IF ERRORLEVEL 2, GOTO ...
IF ERRORLEVEL 1, GOTO ...
```

As an example, if you wanted the following ASK command in your batch file:

```
BE ASK "Run (W)ordPerfect, (L)otus, or
    (Q)uit?", wlq
```

then you might create a batch file that looked like this:

```
:BEGIN
CLS
REM  THIS IS WHERE EACH APPLICATION
WILL LOOP BACK TO AFTER EXITING
BE ASK "Run (W)ordPerfect, (L)otus, or
(Q)uit?", wlq
IF ERRORLEVEL 3 GOTO QUIT
IF ERRORLEVEL 2 GOTO LOTUS
IF ERRORLEVEL 1 GOTO
WORDPERFECT
:WORDPERFECT
CD\WP50
WP
GOTO BEGIN
:LOTUS
CD \LOTUS
123
GOTO BEGIN
:QUIT
```

Because this example contains a total of three items in the key-list, ASK returns one of three ERRORLEVEL codes. Level 1 is returned if you press **W**, level 2 is returned if you press L; and level 3 if you press Q. It does not matter whether you respond with an uppercase Q or lowercase q, as the result is the same.

Directly following the ASK command are three statements controlled by the ERRORLEVEL returned by ASK, which allow a branch to different points within the batch program. The statements are arranged to determine whether the highest ERRORLEVEL has been returned (ERRORLEVEL 3, corresponding to a Q response), then the next highest, and so on, so that ERRORLEVEL 1 is always checked last. Because ERRORLEVEL codes work in *descending* order, always list IF ERRORLEVEL GOTO LABEL *n* statements starting with the far right key in the key-list, and proceed in order to the far left key.

To examine a rather simple, yet effective utilization of BE—ASK, you may want to examine the BEDEMO.BAT file that is found on your original Norton Utilities diskettes.

BE Beep

BE BEEP

Purpose

Plays a tone or a sequence of tones through your computer speaker. You can designate any single tone on the command line or a series of tones in a batch file.

Syntax

BE BEEP [*switches*]

or

BE BEEP [*filespec*][/E]

    filespec   Holds the list of tones you want the computer to play. You cannot use any wild card characters within filespec, but you can include a path name.

Switches

/D*n*	Sets the duration of the requested tone, in 1/18 second.
/F*n*	Specifies the frequency of the tone, where *n* is cycles per second (Hertz).
/R*n*	Repeats the tone *n* times
/W*n*	Waits between tones *n*/18 a second.
/E	Echoes the text in the file specified.

Notes

The frequency of each tone is set by the /F*n* switch. The duration, or length, of each tone is assigned by the /D*n* switch. To repeat a tone, use the /R*n* switch. The /W*n* switch inserts a wait between tones. The /D, /R, and /W switches set the time in 1/18 second.

For example,

BE Beep /F330 /D72 /R5 /W36

plays a 330Hz (cycles per second) tone for four (72/18) seconds, waits two (36/18) seconds, and then repeats that sequence five times (/R5).

You can enter the BEEP switches in any order.

BEEP also can play a continuous series of tones listed in a file. You can enter nontone playing comments in a tone file by beginning the comments with a semicolon (;). BEEP ignores anything listed after a semicolon.

To create a tone file, simply enter the tones in the file just as you enter them on the command line. For example

; A TWO-LINE TONE FILE
/F250 /D48 /R2 /W36
/F550 /D18 /R4 /W36
; YOU CAN ADD COMMENTS IN A
  TONE FILE.

```
; PLACE A SEMICOLON BEFORE
    ANY COMMENTS
```

This tone file repeats a three-second, 250Hz tone twice, waiting two seconds between each repeat, and then immediately plays a 550Hz tone for one second, waiting two seconds between beeps, then plays the beep four times. The / is optional when tones are listed in a tone file. The tone file can look like this, if desired:

```
;  A TWO-LINE TONE FILE
F250 D48 R2 W36
F550 D18 R4 W36
; YOU CAN ADD COMMENTS IN A
    TONE FILE.
; PLACE A SEMICOLON BEFORE
    ANY COMMENTS
```

You can play the TONES file by typing

```
BE BEEP TONES
```

By adding the /E switch and including a comment inside quotation marks, you can incorporate comments into your signalling routine. The /E is available only when imbedded in a batch file. The following example shows a simplified batch file with proper syntax for executing the BE BEEP command with the /E switch set:

```
;Tonefile.bat [Filename]
F250 D48 R1 W36
F550 D18 R1 W36
;"DONE"
;The word DONE will appear on your ;screen
after the two tones have played
```

Execute the following command from the DOS prompt:

```
BE BEEP TONEFILE /E
```

BE Box

BE BOX

Purpose

Draws a rectangle of a requested size and location on your computer screen.

Syntax

BE BOX *top*, *left*, *bottom*, *right* [SINGLE or DOUBLE] [*color*]

top	Specifies the row location of the box's top left corner.
left	Specifies the column location of the box's top left corner.
bottom	Specifies the row location of the box's bottom right corner.
right	Specifies the column location of the box's bottom right corner.
SINGLE	Draws a single width outline box.
DOUBLE	Draws a double width outline box.
color	Specifies the color with which to draw the box.

Note

Picture your screen as a grid, with 80 columns and 24 rows. **BE BOX 0,0,20,79 Single Red** produces a single red box 80 columns wide and 20 rows long.

BE Printchar

BE PRINTCHAR

Purpose

Displays a specified character a specified number of times at the current cursor location.

Syntax

BE PRINTCHAR *character, repetitions* [*color*]

character	Specifies the character to appear.
repetitions	Specifies the number of times the character displays. (The maximum number of times a character can be displayed is 80.)
color	Specifies the color in which the character appears.

Note

You also can specify *intensity* in your color settings. For example, **BE PRINTCHAR T 25 BRIGHT GREEN** prints the character T, 25 times in bright green.

BE Rowcol

BE ROWCOL

Purpose

Positions the cursor at the specified row and column, and optionally displays text.

Syntax

BE ROWCOL *row,col* [*,text*][*color*]

row	Specifies the row to which to move the cursor.
col	Specifies the column to which to move the cursor.
text	Specifies any optional text to appear at the new cursor location. Text must be a continuous string, such as "This_is_a_test," rather than "This is a test."
color	Specifies the color the text appears.

BE Screen Attributes

Purpose

Controls the on-screen appearance of colors and attributes.

Syntax

BE SA *main-setting* [*switches*]

or

BE SA [*intensity*][*foreground*][ON *background*] [*switches*]

intensity	Select from the following: Bright Bold Blinking (Bright and Bold are the same attribute.)
main-setting	Select from the following: Normal Reverse Underline
foreground and *background*	Select from the following: White Black Red Magenta Blue Green Cyan Yellow

You can abbreviate all settings to the first three letters. For example, you can specify Yellow by using "Yel" and Reverse by using "Rev".

Switches

/N	Does not set the border color.
/CLS	Clears the screen after changing color attributes.

Procedures

You can execute the BE SA subcommand from DOS or a batch file.

To execute BE SA from DOS, simply enter the command as described under the Syntax section. For example,

C:> BE SA BRIGHT WHITE ON BLUE

produces a blue background with bright white letters.

The normal rules for creating batch files are in effect. The preceding example, in addition to your own creative ideas, can be incorporated into any batch file.

Notes

Screen Attributes automatically sets the color of the border to match the background color. If you use the /N switch, the border color is not set. If your system is equipped with an EGA card, your computer generates a borderless display.

If you want to have your color choice in Screen Attributes remain in effect, first install the ANSI.SYS driver on your computer.

BE Window

BE WINDOW

Purpose

Draws a window on the computer screen.

Syntax

BE WINDOW *top,left,bottom,right*[*color*] [SHADOW] [ZOOM][EXPLODE]

top   Specifies the row location of the
                         window's top left corner.

left   Specifies the column location of the
                         window's top left corner.

bottom   Specifies the row location of the
                         window's bottom right corner.

right   Specifies the column location of the
                         window's bottom right corner.

color   Specifies the color with which to fill
                         the window.

SHADOW   Draws the window with a see-
                         through shadow.

ZOOM   Zooms the window as it is drawn.

EXPLODE   Explodes the window from the center
                         to user-defined coordinates
                         (functions the same as ZOOM).

Procedures

You can execute the BE WINDOW subcommand from
DOS or incorporate it into your batch files.

To perform a WINDOW subcommand from DOS,
implement the syntax described in this section. For
example,

**C : > BE WINDOW 0,0,24,79 BRIGHT WHITE
ON BLUE EXPLODE SHADOW**

produces a double-line window, with the window itself
beginning in the middle of your display and exploding
outward to its assigned location (the entire display).

Notes

By using BOX, PRINTCHAR, ROWCOL, and
WINDOW in combination, you can create interesting
graphics for your batch programs. For example, you can
draw a window, change the color within the window,
move the cursor to a location within the window, and
then write important text to the screen within the
window (or box). By doing so, you can create your own
alert and dialog boxes.

To examine a batch file that uses not only the WINDOW
function, but a variety of other Norton functions,
examine the MENU.DAT file included on your Norton
disks.

Cursor Size

NCC

Purpose
Changes the cursor size.

Procedures

To change the cursor size:

1. From the DOS prompt, type NCC and press
   Enter.

2. Select Cursor Size and press Enter.

   The control area on the left of your screen
   changes so that you can set the size and shape of
   your cursor.

3. Press the up- or down-arrow keys to toggle the
   lines in the cursor block on and off. Use the left-
   and right-arrow keys to move from the starting
   position to the ending position of the cursor
   block. You can use Tab to move from the
   starting position to the ending position.

4. Press Enter to accept the new size and return to
   the function menu. Press Esc to exit without
   making changes to the cursor.

To return to the default cursor:

Press * from within Cursor Size window.

Notes
The height of the cursor depends on your computer's
display adapter (CGA, EGA, VGA, and so on).

Your computer monitor may display a different cursor than the one displayed. You may need to make several adjustments with the cursor size until you locate the desired shape.

Directory Sort

DS

Purpose

Sorts one or more directories by file name, file extension, time, date, or size.

Syntax

To use the full-screen directory sort:

Type **DS** [*directory name*].

To sort from the DOS command line:

Type **DS** *sort-key(s)* [*directory name*] /S.

Sort-keys include the following:

Name
Extension
Time
Date
Size

Add a minus sign (-) to any sort-key to reverse the sorting order.

Switch

/S   Sorts subdirectories when you run Directory Sort from the DOS command line.

Procedures

Note: Execute the following commands from the DOS prompt.

To sort the current directory:

To sort the current directory by file name, type DS N and press Enter.

To sort the current directory by file date, type DS D and press Enter.

To sort the current directory by file time, type DS T and press Enter.

To sort the current directory by file date and time, type DS DT and press Enter.

To sort the current directory, newest files to the oldest files, type DS D-T- and press Enter.

To sort the entire current drive:

To sort the entire current drive by file name, type DS N \ /S and press Enter.

To sort the entire current drive by file name and extension, type DS NE \ /S and press Enter.

To sort the entire current drive, newest files to the oldest files, type DS D-T- \ /S and press Enter.

To sort the entire current drive by file size, type DS S \ /S and press Enter.

To sort the entire current drive, smallest file to largest in each directory, type DS S- \ /S and press Enter.

To sort the files on drive A:

To sort the files on drive A by file name, type DS N A: and press Enter.

To sort the files on drive A, newest files to the oldest files, type DS D-T- A: /S and press Enter.

To sort the files in a particular subdirectory:

To sort the DOS directory by file name, type DS N \DOS and press Enter.

To run Directory Sort interactively:

1. Type **DS** and press **Enter**.

2. Select **C**hange Sort Order.

3. Select how you want the files sorted: **N**ame, **E**xtension, **D**ate, **T**ime, or **S**ize. Use a minus sign for reverse sorting.

4. Select **R**esort.

5. Select **W**rite to write the changes to your disk.

6. Press **Esc** or **F10** to leave Directory Sort.

To move a file or files:

1. Type **DS** and press **Enter**.

2. Highlight the file(s) you want to move. Press the space bar to select each file.

3. Select **M**ove File(s).

4. Move the file(s) to a new location by using the cursor-movement keys and pressing **Enter**.

5. Select **W**rite Changes to Disk.

Notes

Do not turn off your computer as Directory Sort is running. Doing so can damage the logical order of your disk. To interrupt Directory Sort, press Ctrl-Break.

You can run Directory Sort from the DOS command line or interactively. If you run the Directory Sort from the DOS command line, after the sorting is complete, you return to the DOS command line.

When running Directory Sort interactively, you can use any of these keys to scroll through the file list:

↑	Scrolls up one line.
↓	Scrolls down one line.
PgUp	Scrolls up one page.
PgDn	Scrolls down one page.

Home   Moves to the beginning of the file
                        listing.

End   Moves to the end of the file listing.

You can include more than one sort-key when you
create a sort request.

If you run Directory Sort interactively, you can move
individual files or groups of files to any position within
the current directory. For example, you can move the
file called MYWORK to the top of the directory, making
it appear always as the first file in the directory.

Disk Information, DI

DI

Purpose

Reports advanced technical information about a disk,
including the media type, number of sides, the number
of sectors per track, the number of clusters, the number
of bytes per sector, and the number of sectors in the File
Allocation Table.

Syntax

DI [*d*:]

d: is the letter of the drive you want to obtain disk
information.

Procedures

To obtain disk information about drive C:

From the DOS prompt, type DI C: and press Enter.

To obtain disk information about drive A:

From the DOS prompt, type DI A: and press Enter.

Notes

Disk Information reports considerable information about
the disk in the specified drive. DOS reports some of the

information, and the disk's boot record reports other
parts of the information. The following information is
reported when you run Disk Information:

System ID	The operating system that was used to format the disk.
Media descriptor	A hexadecimal value that indicates what type of disk is in the drive. The typical values include:
F0	A 1.4M 3 1/2-inch diskette.
F8	A hard disk.
F9	A 1.2M 5 1/4-inch diskette or a 720K 3 1/2-inch diskette.
FD	A 360K 5 1/4-inch diskette.
FE	A 160K 5 1/4-inch diskette.
FFA	320K 5 1/4-inch diskette.
Drive number	0 equals A, 1 equals drive B, and so on.
Bytes per sector	The total number of bytes per second, usually 512.
Sectors per cluster	DOS always creates files in multiple-sector units, which are called clusters. The number of sectors per cluster varies, based on media type and the operating system version.
Number of FATs	All versions of DOS should contain 2 FATs (File Allocation Table), and all media other than RAM disks. For RAM disks, the number can be 2 or 1, depending on the RAM disk driver.

Root directory entries	The number of files and subdirectories that can be stored in the root directory, which varies with media type and operating system revision.
Sectors per FAT	Varies with media type.
Number of clusters	The number of clusters in the DOS partition. This figure, which varies according to media type, is useful for determining which type of FAT is in use. Disks having 4,085 or fewer clusters have FATs with 12-bit entries. Those disks with more than 4,085 clusters have 16-bit FATs.
Number of sectors	The total number of sectors on a disk is equal to the sum of the number of clusters times the number of sectors per cluster and the number of sectors in the DOS system area.
Offset to FAT	The sector in which the first File Allocation Table begins.
Offset to directory	The sector number where the root directory begins on the disk.
Offset to data	The sector number where the data area on the disk begins.
Sectors per track	The number of sectors varies according to the media type being checked. The common sectors are 9 for a 360K diskette or a 720K 3 1/2-inch diskette; 15 for a 1.2M 5 1/4-

inch diskette; 17 for most hard disks; or 18 for a 1.4M 3 1/2-inch diskette.

Sides

The total number of logical sides on the disk.

Hidden sectors

Number indicates the starting sector number of the DOS partition. (The first sector on the disk is sector 0.)

═Disk Information, NU

NU

Purpose

Provides disk information such as basic storage capacity and logical dimensions, and a map of disk usage.

Procedures

Note: Execute the following commands from the DOS prompt.

To display a disk map of the current drive:

1. Type **NU** and press **Enter**.

2. Select **D**isk information.

3. Select **M**ap Disk Usage.

4. Press **Esc** twice to return to the Main Menu.

To display a technical report about your disk drive:

1. ´Type **NU** and press **Enter**.

2. Select **D**isk information.

3. Select **T**echnical information to see a report on the characteristics of your disk drive.

4. Press **Esc** twice to return to the Main Menu.

To display a disk map of drive A:

1. Type **NU** and press **Enter**.

2. Select **E**xplore disk.

3. Select **C**hoose Item.

4. Select **C**hange Drive and press **A**.

5. Press **Esc** twice to return to the Main Menu.

6. Select **D**isk Information.

7. Select **M**ap Disk Usage.

8. Press **Esc** twice to return to the Main Menu.

To display a technical report about drive A:

1. Type **NU** and press **Enter**.

2. Select **E**xplore Disk.

3. Select **C**hoose Item.

4. Select **C**hange Drive and press **A**.

5. Press **Esc** twice.

6. Select **D**isk Information.

7. Select **T**echnical Information.

Disk Test

DT

Purpose

Checks a diskette or disk drive for any kind of damage.
During the checking process, Disk Text can repair any
repairable damage, mark good sectors as bad or bad
sectors as good, and move data currently located in
questionable clusters to a safe location.

Syntax

DT [*d*:][*filespec*][*switches*]

d: The letter of the drive you want to
       examine and test.

filespec	The specified files you want to examine.
switches	The available switches you can use with Disk Test.

Switches

/B	Performs both a disk test and a file test.
/Cn	Marks cluster n as bad.
/Cn-	Marks cluster n as good.
/D	Tests the entire disk for damage.
/F	Tests all files on the disk for damage.
/LOG	Formats output messages to be suitable for printing or logging to a file.
/M	Moves questionable clusters to a safe location and marks the questionable clusters as bad.
/S	Tests files in subdirectories when a filespec is specified.

Procedures

Note: Execute the following commands from the DOS prompt.

To run Disk Test on the current drive:

1. Type **DT** and press **Enter**.
2. Select **D**isk-read, **F**ile-read, or **B**oth.

To run Disk Test on drive B:

To run Disk Test on drive B and test all files, type **DT B: /F** and press **Enter**.

Disk Test reports any errors located as it reads the files. To move the clusters reported with errors by Disk Test to a new, safe location, run DT again with the /M switch.

To run Disk Test on drive B, test all files, and move clusters located in questionable areas to a safe location, type DT B: /F/M and press Enter.

Disk Test locates and marks bad clusters, and moves the data to a safe location.

To test a specific group of files for bad clusters:

To test all .WP files on drive A for bad clusters, type DT A:*.WP and press Enter.

Because this command is running the file test, you do not need to add the /F switch when a filespec is included.

To mark and unmark a specific cluster as bad:

To mark a specific cluster (1951) as bad, type DT /C1951 and press Enter.

To unmark a specific cluster (1951) as bad, type DT /C1951- and press Enter.

Notes

If you issue DT without any parameters, you are prompted for appropriate switches (such as Disk Read, File Read or Both).

Disk Test tests a drive for physical damage, and determines whether data can be read from the disk without errors.

Disk Test is much more comprehensive than the DOS CHKDSK command.

If File-read test (/F) is performed and errors are located, Disk Test may report DANGER NOW or DANGER TO COME. Use Disk Test to move the data to another place on the disk and to mark the sector as bad.

If a sector is marked as bad, you are not in danger of losing important data because DOS ignores the bad sector, and does not store any data in that sector.

Should a problem be located in the disk's system area, such as the boot record, file allocation table, or root directory, you are in danger of losing all the data on the disk. Copy the disk using the DOS COPY command and then reformat the disk. If errors are still reported, discard the floppy disk.

Note: Do not use DISKCOPY because DISKCOPY also copies problem areas.

═ DOS Colors ═══════════

NCC

Purpose

Changes DOS colors.

Procedures

To change the DOS colors:

1. From the DOS prompt, type **NCC** and press **Enter**.

2. Select DOS Colors.

    Three color charts are displayed in the control area, along with a block of example text on the right of your screen. These three charts are labeled Foreground, Background, and Border. Only one chart is active at a time. The title bar of the active chart is displayed in reverse video.

3. Use the up-arrow key, down-arrow key, or Tab key to move from one chart to another. Use the right- and left-arrow keys to change the selected color within the active chart. The current color selection is indicated by an arrow.

4. Press **Enter** to place changes into effect and exit. Press **Esc** to exit without making changes to the DOS colors.

5. Press **Esc** to exit to DOS.

To restore DOS color default settings:
Press *from within the DOS Colors window.

Explore Disk

NU

Purpose
Enables you to explore the disk and to examine, edit, search, and copy disk information.

Procedures
Note: Execute the following commands from the DOS prompt.

To choose a file in The Norton Utilities Main Program:
1. Type NU and press Enter.
2. Select Explore Disk.
3. Select Choose Item.
4. Select File.
5. Use the cursor-movement keys to highlight the desired file and press Enter.
6. Select either Display Information or Edit/display item.

To choose a cluster in The Norton Utilities Main Program:
1. Type NU and press Enter.
2. Select Explore Disk.
3. Select Choose Item.
4. Select c Luster.
5. Type the beginning cluster range and press Enter.
6. Type the ending cluster range and press Enter.

To choose a sector in The Norton Utilities Main Program:

1. Type NU and press Enter.

2. Select Explore Disk.

3. Select Choose Item.

4. Select Sector.

5. Type the beginning sector range and press Enter.

6. Type the ending sector range and press Enter.

To choose an absolute sector in The Norton Utilities Main Program

1. Type NU and press Enter.

2. Select Explore Disk.

3. Select Choose Item.

4. Select Absolute Sector.

5. Type the side, cylinder, starting sector number, the total number of the absolute sector, and press Enter.

To view the FAT of your disk:

1. Type NU and press Enter.

2. Select Explore Disk.

3. Select the type of item you want to explore by selecting Choose Item.

4. Select Change Directory and press Home.

The root directory is highlighted.

5. Press Enter and then choose the File option.

6. Select Edit/Display Item.

To view information on a selected item:

1. Type NU and press Enter.

2. Select Explore Disk.

3. Select the type of item you want to explore by selecting Choose Item.

4. Select I nformation on Item.

To search your disk for data:

1. Type NU and press Enter.

2. Select E xplore Disk.

3. Select S earch Item/Disk for Data.

4. Select T ext to Search For.

5. Type the text to search for and press Enter.

6. Choose S tart Search.

Notes

Do not write or edit the FAT (File Allocation Table),
Partition Table, or DOS System Area unless you are
absolutely certain you understand the procedure.
Because this area of your computer is highly technical,
any error you make can prevent your computer from
working. Always back up the entire disk before editing
or writing to the FAT, Partition Table, or DOS System
Area.

Use of The Norton Utilities Main Program by
inexperienced computer users can cause irreversible
damage to data and files. This book is not intended as a
replacement for the documentation that is included with
your copy of Norton Utilities. Please refer to the
documentation to obtain extensive technical information
about The Norton Utilities Main Program.

Always make a backup copy of your disk before writing
or editing any section of your disk with The Norton
Utilities Main Program.

File Attributes

FA

Purpose

Displays, sets, or resets any of the four DOS file
attributes: Archive, Hidden, System, and Read-Only.
Similar to the DOS ATTRIB command.

Syntax

FA [*filespec*] [*attribute switches*] [*switches*]

filespec	The specified files you want to examine.
attribute switches	The attribute you want to change.
switches	The available switches you can use with File Attributes.

Attribute Switches

/A	Archive.
/HID	Hidden.
/R	Read-only.
/SYS	System.

Switches

/CLEAR	Clears (removes) all file attributes.
/P	Pauses display after each full screen. (The screen also pauses if you press any key.)
/S	Includes subdirectories in the file search that match the filespec.
/T	Shows totals only.
/U	Shows all unusual files (those files that have the attributes already set).

Procedures

> _Note:_ Execute the following commands from the DOS prompt.

To see a listing of file attributes:

To see a listing of the attributes of all files, type FA and press Enter.

To see a listing of all files with the system attribute, type FA /SYS and press Enter.

To hide files:

To hide all files in the current directory, type FA / HID+ and press Enter.

To hide all files on drive A, type FA A:*.* /HID+ and press Enter.

To hide all files with the extension .TXT, type FA *.TXT /HID+ and press Enter.

To hide all files in the current directory and its subdirectories, type FA /HID+/S and press Enter.

To unhide files:

To unhide all files in the current directory, type FA /HID- and press Enter.

To unhide all files on drive A, type FA A:*.* /HID- and press Enter.

To unhide all files in the current directory and its subdirectories, type FA /HID-/S and press Enter.

To make files read only:

To make all files read only, type FA /R+ and press Enter.

To remove read only from marked files, type FA /R- and press Enter.

To make all system files read only, type FA /SYS/ R+ and press Enter.

To make files archive:

To make all files archive, type FA /A+ and press Enter.

To remove archive from all marked files, type FA / A- and press Enter.

Notes

To set a file attribute, add + (the plus sign) to the attribute switches. To reset the file attribute, add - (the minus sign) to the attribute switches. For example:

/HID+	Adds the Hidden attribute to the file.
/HID-	Resets the Hidden attribute to the file.

Do not put a space between the attribute switch and the + or - sign.

Wrong:	/HID +
Correct:	/HID+

File Date

FD

Purpose

Sets, clears, or resets the date or the time stamp on a DOS-created file.

Syntax

FD *filespec* [*switches*]

filespec	The specified files you want to examine.
switches	The available switches you can use with File Date.

Switches

/S	Includes the subdirectories in the search for files that match the filespec.
/P	Pauses display after each screen. (Pressing any key also pauses the display.)
/D*date*	Specifies the date to appear in the files.
/T*time*	Specifies the time to appear in the files.

Using /0 with no date gives no date or time on files specified.

Issue the FD command alone to use the current date and time.

Procedures

Note: Execute the following commands from the DOS prompt.

To reset the date:

To reset the date on all files on the drive to the current date, type FD and press Enter.

To reset the date to the current date for all files on drive A, type FD A: and press Enter.

To reset the date of all .EXE files on the current drive to 12-25-90, type FD *.EXE /d12-25-90 and press Enter.

To clear the date on all files on drive A, type FD A: /D and press Enter.

To reset the time:

To reset the time of all .COM files in the DOS directory to 9:00 a.m., type FD \DOS*.COM / T09:00:00 and press Enter.

Notes

If no date appears when you use the /D switch, the date is cleared. Always specify the date as mmddyy (for example, July 19, 1990 is 071990).

If no time appears when you use the /T switch, the time is cleared. Always specify the time as hh:mm:ss (for example, 10:15 a.m. is 10:15:00).

File Find

FF

Purpose

Locates lost files or directories by searching through all directories of one or more disks, or prints a complete file catalog of an entire disk.

Syntax

FF [*d*:][*filename*][*switches*]

d:	The letter of the drive you want to search.
filename	The name of the file you want to find.
switches	The available switches you can use with File Find.

Switches

/A	Searches for all files on all drives.
/P	Pauses the display after each screen of information. (Pressing any key also pauses the display.)
/W	Lists files in a wide display format.

Procedures

Note: Execute the following commands from the DOS prompt.

To find files on the current drive:

To find a file called REPORT.MAY on the current drive, type **FF REPORT.MAY** and press Enter.

To find all files and subdirectories with the name REPORT on the current drive, type **FF REPORT** and press Enter.

To find files on a specific drive:

To find a file called REPORT.MAY on drive A, type **FF A:REPORT.MAY** and press Enter.

To find files of a particular type:

To find all .EXE files on drive A, type **FF A:*.EXE** and press Enter.

To find all .EXE file on drive C, type **FF C:*.EXE** and press Enter.

To find all .COM files on all drives, type **FF *.COM /A** and press Enter.

To see all files:

To see all the files on the current drive, type **FF** and press Enter.

To see all files on drive A, type **FF A:** and press Enter.

To see all files on the current drive in a wide-display format, type **FF /W** and press Enter.

To see all files on all drives in a wide-display format, type **FF /A/W** and press Enter.

To see all files on all drives with a pause after each screen, type **FF /A/P** and press Enter.

To see all files of a particular type:

To see all .WKS files on all drives with a pause after each screen, type **FF *.WKS /A/P** and press Enter.

To see all .EXE files on all drives in a wide-display format, type **FF *.EXE /A/W** and press Enter.

To print a list of all files:

To print a list of files on the current drive, type **FF >
PRN** and press **Enter** .

To print a list of files on drive A, type **FF A: > PRN**
and press **Enter**.

To print a list of files of a particular type:

To print a list of .EXE files on the current drive,
type **FF *.EXE > PRN** and press **Enter**.

To print a list of .EXE files on drive C, type **FF
C:*.EXE > PRN** and press **Enter**.

Notes

You can stop the search for a file or directory at any
time by pressing **Ctrl-Break** or **Esc**.

Each matching file is displayed with the file or
directory's name, size, time, and date of the file's
creation or modification.

If no extension is included on the command line, File
Find searches for all files with the file name, regardless
of the extension.

You can pause the screen at any time by pressing the
space bar. Press the space bar again to continue the
listing.

File Find locates both Hidden and System files.

If no file name is specified, a listing of all files on the
drive is displayed under their appropriate subdirectories
by File Find.

You can use the standard DOS wild cards, * and ?, to
specify a file name.

Do not include a path as part of the file name. File Find
automatically searches the entire disk for the requested
file or directory name.

When you do not specify a drive, File Find searches the
current drive.

File Info

FI

Purpose

Attaches a description or comment to a file and directory name in a directory listing. Views a directory listing with all attached descriptions and comments.

Syntax

FI [*filespec*][*comment*][*switches*]

filespec	The specified files you want to examine.
comment	The comment you want to attach.
switches	The available switches you can use with File Information.

Switches

/C	Lists only those files with comments attached.
/D	Deletes a comment.
/E	Edits or enters a comment.
/L	Lists long comments in entirety.
/P	Pauses the display after each screen of information. (Pressing any key also pauses the display.)
/Pack	Compresses the FILEINFO.FI file.
/S	Includes subdirectories in directory listing.

Procedures

Note: Execute the following commands from the DOS prompt.

To view files in the current directory:

To view the current directory, type FI and press Enter

To view only the files with comments in the current directory, type FI /C and press Enter.

To view files on a specific drive:

To view drive A with comments, type FI A: and press Enter.

To view only the files with comments on drive A, type FI A: /C and press Enter.

To view files in a specific directory:

To view the files in the LOTUS directory on the current drive, type FI \LOTUS and press Enter.

To view only the files with comments in the LOTUS directory on the current drive, type FI \LOTUS /C and press Enter.

To view the files in the LOTUS directory on drive A, type FI A:\LOTUS and press Enter.

To view only the files with comments in the LOTUS directory on drive A, type FI A:\LOTUS /C and press Enter.

To view files of a particular type:

To view the .TXT files in the current directory, type FI *.TXT and press Enter.

To view only the .TXT files with comments in the current directory, type FI *.TXT /C and press Enter.

To view only the .TXT files on drive A, type FI A:*.TXT and press Enter.

To view only the .TXT files with comments on drive A, type FI A:*.TXT /C and press Enter.

To add a comment to a particular file:

To add a comment to the file REPORT.TXT located in the current drive, do the following:

1. Type **FI REPORT.TXT /E** and press **Enter**.

2. When the Comment Dialog Box appears, type your file comment.

3. Press **Enter** to attach the comment and complete the comment entry.

To add a comment to a group of files:

To add a comment to all .WKS files located in the drive A, do the following:

1. Type **FI A:*.WKS /E** and press **Enter**.

2. When the Comment Dialog Box appears, type your file comment.

3. Press **Enter** to attach the comment and complete the Comment entry.

4. The Comment dialog box appears for the next file. Repeat Steps 2 and 3.

To delete a comment from a particular file:

To delete a comment from the REPORT.TXT file located in the current drive, type **FI REPORT.TXT /D** and press **Enter**.

To delete all comments from all files:

To delete all comments from all files located in the current drive, do the following:

1. Type **FI /D** and press **Enter**.

2. Type **Y** to confirm the deletion of the comments.

To delete all comments from a particular group of files:

To delete the comments from all .WKS files located on drive A, do the following:

1. Type **FI A:*.WKS /D** and press **Enter**.

2. Type **Y** to confirm the deletion of the comments.

To display a list of files:

To display a list of files with complete comments in the current drive, type **FI /L** and press **Enter**.

To display a list of files with complete comments in drive A, type **FI A: /L** and press **Enter**.

To display a list of all .WKS files with complete comments in drive A, type **FI A:*.WKS /L** and press **Enter**.

To add a comment to a file:

To add the comment "Fred's Proposal" to the file LETTER.TXT from the DOS command line, type **FI LETTER.TXT Fred's Proposal** and press **Enter**.

To pack the FILEINFO.FI file:

Type **FI /PACK** and press **Enter**.

Notes

FI is similar to the DOS DIR command. If you use the FI command instead of DIR, you can pause the directory listing at anytime by pressing the **space bar**. To resume the directory listing, press the **space bar** again. If you pause the listing, you can press **Enter** to see one additional file at a time. Press any other key to resume the continuous display.

Use the following keys when you use the FI command:

Esc or **F10**	Quits the directory listing.
space bar	Pauses the screen, then again to get another screen.
Enter	Enables you to see one file at a time when the screen is paused.
Any key	Resumes continuous display of the files.

When editing comments, File Info displays an editing box in which you can either add a comment or edit an existing comment. When editing a comment, you can use the following keys:

Ctrl-→	Moves cursor right one word.
Ctrl-F	Moves cursor right one word.
Ctrl-←	Moves cursor left one word.
Ctrl-A	Moves cursor left one word.
Home	Moves cursor to beginning of the line.
End	Moves cursor to end of the line.
→	Moves cursor right one character.
Ctrl-D	Moves cursor right one character.
←	Moves cursor left one character.
Ctrl-S	Moves cursor left one character.
Backspace	Deletes one character left of cursor.
Delete	Deletes one character under the cursor.
Ctrl-T	Deletes one word right of the cursor.
Ctrl-W	Deletes one word left of the cursor.
Ctrl-Y	Deletes the entire line.
Esc	Aborts or erases any added text.

A comment can contain a maximum of 65 characters.

If you use the /L switch, all 65 characters are displayed.

You can edit or change the comment of files with different names by using the /E switch without a specific file name. After adding or editing a comment, File Info moves to the next file on the list. Press **Esc** at anytime to quit.

You can use the standard DOS wild cards, * and ?, to specify a file name.

Use the /S switch to use File Find in both the current directory and subdirectories.

When you create or edit comments with File Find, a special file called FILEINFO.FI is created and changed. You cannot directly access or alter this file. FILEINFO.FI holds the file comments you create. If you delete a large number of comments, you can speed up this file by using the /PACK switch.

═ File Size ══════════════════════════════════

FS

Purpose

Displays the size of one file, the size of many files, or the total size of all the files within a directory. File Size also determines the percentage of slack for the specified files, and reports whether a group of files will fit onto a target disk.

Syntax

FS [*filespec*][*target-drive*:][*switches*]

filespec	The specified files you want to examine.
target-drive	The drive on which the files are located.
switches	The available switches you can use with File Size.

Switches

/P	Pauses display after each screen. (This command is similar to the DOS DIR /P command. Pressing any key also pauses the display.)
/S	Includes subdirectories for files that match filespec.
/T	Displays only totals and does not list the size of individual files.

Procedures

Note: Execute the following commands from the DOS prompt.

To display a listing of file sizes:

To display a size listing of all files in the current directory, type FS and press Enter .

To display a size listing of all files in the current directory and all its subdirectories, type FS /S and press Enter .

To display a size listing of all the .COM files located in the root directory, type FS *.COM and press Enter.

To learn the total space used by .COM files:

To learn the total space used by .COM files located in the root directory, type FS *.COM /T and press Enter.

To learn the total space used by all the .COM files in the DOS directory, type FS \DOS*.COM /T and press Enter.

To learn the total space used by all the .COM files located on the entire disk, type FS *.COM /S/T and press Enter.

To learn whether all the .COM files located in the DOS directory on drive C will fit on drive A, type FS \DOS*.COM A: /S/T and press Enter.

To learn whether all the .COM files on drive C will fit on drive A, type FS *.COM A: /S/T and press Enter.

To display file sizes on the entire disk:

To display the size of all directories on the disk and the total size of all the files on the disk and the overall slack on the disk, type FS \ /T /S and press Enter.

Notes

If you include a target-drive specification in the FS command, File Size checks to see whether the target drive has enough space available to hold the files.

Slack is the amount of free space DOS does not use in a cluster when a file occupies a disk. For example, if your computer uses clusters of 1024 bytes and you store a file of 1025 bytes, DOS stores the file in two clusters. DOS uses 2048 bytes of space to store 1025 bytes of data.

Format Recover

FR

Purpose

Recovers an accidentally reformatted hard disk.

Syntax

FR [*d*:][/SAVE][/NOBAK]

d: is the letter of the drive you want to recover.

Switches

/SAVE   Saves the necessary information to
               do a format recovery and complete
               the file recovery.

/NOBAK   Does not create the file backup file,
               FRECOVER.BAK.

Procedures

Note: Execute the following commands from the
DOS prompt.

To run Format Recover:

1. Type **FR** and press **Enter**.

2. Select the desired option from the pop-up box.

To run Format Recover and store the information to recover drive D:

Type **FR D: /SAVE** and press **Enter**.

To recover an accidentally reformatted Drive C:

1. Type **FR** and press **Enter**.

2. Select Restore Disk Information if you used FR
   to create a FRECOVER.DAT file.

   Select Unformat Disk if you did not use FR to
   create a FRECOVER.DAT file.

Notes

FR creates a file called FRECOVER.DAT, which is
used to store the necessary information to recover a hard
disk. Each time you run FR with the /SAVE switch,
FRECOVER.DAT is updated. You easily can run FR
with the /SAVE switch from your AUTOEXEC.BAT
file, ensuring constant updating. Other Norton Utilities
can use the information stored in FRECOVER.DAT to
recover files. Although FRECOVER.DAT is not
required to recover files, the recovery operation is much
smoother if the file is available.

Use Format Recover on hard drive systems only.

Keyboard Rate

NCC

Purpose

Sets the repeat speed of the keys and the amount of time the computer pauses before beginning to repeat the keys. This menu option is available from The Norton Control Center.

Procedures

To change the keyboard rate of your computer:

1. At the DOS prompt, type NCC and press Enter.

2. Select Keyboard Rate.

3. Use the left- or right-arrow keys to specify the number of characters that appear when a key is held down for one second after the delay period. (The setting appears at the top of the screen.)

4. Use either the up- or down-arrow key to change the amount of time before a key begins to repeat. (This setting appears in the lower center of the screen.)

   You can test the changes you make to your keyboard by typing text. The text appears in a small field at the bottom of your screen.

5. Press Enter to accept the changes and return to the menu. Press Esc to exit without making any changes.

6. Press Esc to exit NCC.

To restore the keyboard to its original speed:

Press * from within the Keyboard Rate window.

Note

You can specify the keyboard rate through the Norton Control Center on AT-type computers only (those personal computers that operate with 80286 and 80386 processors).

Line Print

LP

Purpose

Prints text files with a variety of formatting options, including line and page numbers, headers, margins, and page size. Line Print can print files using the EBCDIC code, WordStar files, and send a setup string to the printer before printing starts.

Line Print provides an easy way to print any text file to a printer, file, or device. Line Print is especially handy when you need line numbers added on the text, such as a program listings. To add line number, use the /N switch in the command line.

Syntax

LP *filespec* [*where-to-print*][*switches*]

filespec	The file or files to print.
where-to-print	The device location, such as LPT1 or COM2.

Switches

/T*n*	Top margin, number of lines. Has a default value of 3.
/B*n*	Bottom margin, number of lines. Has a default value of 5.
/L*n*	Left margin, number of columns. Has a default value of 5.
/R*n*	Right margin, number of columns. Has a default value of 5.
/H*n*	Height of page in lines. Has a default value of 66.

/W*n*	Width of page in columns. Has a default value of 85.
/S*n*	Line Spacing. Has a default value of 1.
/P*n*	Starting Page number. Has a default value of 1.
/N	Use this switch when you want line numbering. Has default value set at off.
/80	Sets 80-column print width. Has default value set at on.
/132	Sets 132-column (condensed) print. Has default setting of off.
/HEADER*n*	Sets type of header. Has default value of 1. *n*=0:no headers; *n*=1:current date and time; *n*=2:current date and time plus file date and time
/EBCDIC	Tells LP file is encoded in EBCDIC, rather than ASCII. Has default setting of off.
/WS	Prints Wordstar files. Characters in the IBM PC extended character set (ASCII 128-255) are not printed. Has default setting of off.
/SET:*filespec*	Sends the setup string found in filespec to the printer before printing. Has default setting of none.

If the /SET:*filespec* option is used, all the control codes (called the setup string) found in the specified file, are sent to the printer before printing begins. The control codes are listed in the file in the same format as those used in the Lotus 1-2-3 setup string command. Each setup string can take one of these three forms:

\nnn   nnn is the decimal number for the code you want to send. Because three digits are required, be sure that you use leading zeros as required.

\C   C is the control character to send.

C   C is any character to send.

Just as with Lotus 1-2-3, you can string the control codes together in one line, one after the other.

For example,

    \AThis is a test!\013\010

sends a Ctrl-A(ASCII 001) to the printer, followed by the letters "This is a test!", a carriage return, and a line-feed.

The Norton setup string enables you to separate control codes by carriage returns. For example, the preceding string can also appear in the file as

    \AThis is a
    test!\013
    \010

Control codes separated by carriage returns are easier to read. If you need to send a carriage return to the printer as part of the setup string, you must do so by preceding the ASCII value with the \ character.

Procedures

Note: Execute the following commands from the DOS prompt.

To print a file:

To print the file TEST.DOC, type LP TEST.DOC and press Enter.

To print a file in a specific format:

To print the file TEST.DOC in Wordstar format,
type **LP TEST.DOC /WS** and press **Enter**.

To print a file in a specific print mode on an IBM-compatible printer:

To print the file TEST.DOC in compressed print
mode, type **LP TEST.DOC /132** and press **Enter**.

To print a file with numbered lines on an IBM-compatible printer:

To print the file TEST.DOC with all lines
numbered, type **LP TEST.DOC /N** and press
Enter.

To print the file TEST.DOC in compressed print
mode and to number all lines in the file, type **LP
TEST.DOC /132/N** and press **Enter**.

To print a file starting at a specific page number:

To print the file TEST.DOC starting page number
15, type **LP TEST.DOC /P15** and press **Enter**.

To print a file double-spaced:

To print the file TEST.DOC double-spaced, type **LP
TEST.DOC /S2** and press **Enter**.

To print the file TEST.DOC double-spaced and with
all lines numbered, type **LP TEST.DOC /L2/N** and
press **Enter**.

Notes

A new line on the IBM PC actually consists of two
characters: a carriage return-ASCII 013-followed by a
line-feed- ASCII 010.)

Line Print can print more than one file at a time, by
using the standard DOS wild card characters, * and ?.

To print files encoded into EBCDIC or Wordstar format,
use either the /EBCDIC or /WordStar format. If you are
using Wordstar or any other word processor that attaches

a special meaning to the eighth bit, use the /WS switch to suppress the use of the eighth bit.

Create your own batch files that contain Line Print commands to save yourself time and to prevent typing errors.

List Directories

LD

Purpose

Lists all directories in either a graphic, or diagram, style or in a text format. List Directories is used to print or create a file of the structure of your directories on the disk.

Syntax

LD [*d*:][*pathname*][*switches*]

d	The drive that contains the directories you want to list.
pathname	The pathname to the directory.
switches	The available switches you can use with List Directories.

Switches

/A	Lists the directories of all the drives on the computer.
/G	Displays the directories in a graphic or diagram style.
/N	Suppresses printing of extended IBM graphics characters on non-IBM printers.
/P	Pauses the display after each full screen. (Pressing any key also pauses the display.)

/T   Displays the total number and size of
                        all the files in each directory on the
                        drive.

Procedures

Note: Execute the following commands from the
DOS prompt.

To display a list of directories:

To display a list of directories on the default drive,
type **LD** and press **Enter**.

To display a list of all directories on drive A, type
LD A: and press **Enter**.

To display and pause a list of all directories on the
default drive, type **LD /P** and press **Enter** to
advance one line, or press the **space bar** to see the
next screen of information.

To display a graphic list of directories:

To display a graphic list of all directories on the
default drive, type **LD /G** and press **Enter**.

To display a graphic list of all directories on drive
A, type **LD A: /G** and press **Enter**.

To display and pause a graphic list of all directories
on the default drive, type **LD /G/P** and press **Enter**.

To print a list of directories:

To display and print a list of all directories on the
default drive, type **LD > prn:** and press **Enter**.

To print a graphic list of directories on printers that support extended IBM characters:

To display and print a graphic list of all directories
on the default drive, type **LD /G > prn:** and press
Enter.

●

To display and print a graphic list of all directories
on the default drive to a printer that does not support
extended IBM characters, type LD /G/N > prn: and
press Enter.

To total the number and size of all files:

To display a list and total the number and size of all
files in each directory on the default drive, type
LD /T and press Enter.

To display a list and total the number and size of all
files in each directory on drive A, type LD A: /T
and press Enter.

Note

List Directories is similar to the DOS TREE command,
but has the added feature of a graphic display.

Norton Change Directory

NCD

Purpose

Offers two ways of moving through and using extensive
directory structures. Enables you to change a directory
without specifying the entire path name. This command
displays a full-screen, scrollable graphic that enables
you to make, change, rename, and remove directories.

Syntax

NCD MD [*directory name*]

   or

NCD RD [*directory name*]

   or

NCD [*end-point directory name*][*switches*]

Switches

/R	Rescans the disk directory.
/N	Does not write TREEINFO.NCD.

Procedures

Note: Execute the following commands from the DOS prompt.

To view a graphic tree of the directory structure:

Type **NCD** and press **Enter**.

To create a specific directory:

To make a directory called REPORTS from the command line, type **NCD MD REPORTS** and press **Enter**.

To make a directory called REPORTS within NCD, do the following:

1. Type **NCD** and press **Enter**.
2. Move the highlight bar to the position where you want to add the directory.
3. Press **F7**.
4. Type **REPORTS** and press **Enter**.

To change to a specific directory:

To change the directory to LOTUS, type **NCD LOTUS** or **NCD LOT** or **NCD L** and press **Enter**.

To change to the root of the current drive, type **NCD ** and press **Enter**.

To change the directory to A:\LETTERS, type **NCD A:\LETTERS** or **NCD A:\LET** or **NCD A:\L** and press **Enter**.

To rename a directory:

1. Type **NCD** and press **Enter**.
2. Use the cursor-movement keys to highlight the directory you want renamed.

3. Press F6 to rename the directory.

4. Type the name of the new directory.

5. Press Enter.

To perform other operations:

To rescan the drive, type NCD /R and press Enter.

or

From within NCD, press F2 (Rescan). When complete, press F10 (Quit) to exit.

To use NCD and not write to the file TREEINFO.NCD, type NCD /N and press Enter.

Notes

The Norton Change Directory uses the TREEINFO.NCD file to store the information about your directories on the drive. If you make or remove directories with the DOS MD or RD commands, Norton Change Directory must reread the directory and store the information in the TREEINFO.NCD file. Use either the /R switch or F3 to have Norton Change Directory reread the directory.

To use The Norton Change Directory on a write-protected diskette, use the /N switch. The /N switch prevents an error message from occurring.

When using The Norton Change Directory, you do not need to type the full DOS path to move through the directory tree. For example, assume that you had this directory set on your disk

\WP\REPORTS\DON

To use the DOS Change Directory Command, you must type

CD\WP\REPORTS\DON

Using The Norton Change Directory Command, you need only type

NCD DON

If the subdirectory DON is the only directory on the
drive starting with the letter D, you can abbreviate the
command further by only typing

  NCD D

You can use The Norton Change Directory command to
rapidly move through the directory structure by only
typing the end-point directory.

Move through The Norton Change Directory by using
the cursor-movement keys. You also can use PgUp or
PgDn to scroll through the graphic display. Press Home
to scroll to the beginning of the display. Press End to
scroll to the end of the display.

By typing the name of a directory, The Norton Change
Directory rapidly moves the highlight bar to that
directory. Press Ctrl-Enter to find the next match.

Function Keys

You can use these function keys in The Norton Change
Directory:

F1 accesses Help.

F2 rescans the selected drive and update the graphic
directory tree and the TREEINFO.NCD file.
(Pressing F2 is the equivalent to using the /R
switch.)

F3 change drives. When a dialog box appears, select
a drive using the cursor-movement keys, and then
press Enter. Press Esc to clear the dialog box
without changing the current drive.

F6 renames a directory. Move the highlight bar to
the directory to rename, press F6, and type the new
name of the directory, then press Enter.

F7 creates a new directory directly under the one
highlighted by the selection bar. After pressing F7,
type the new directory name, and press Enter.

F8 deletes the directory under the directory selection bar. Press F8 to delete the directory. As with DOS, the directory must be empty before you can delete it with The Norton Change Directory.

F9 changes the number of lines on the display. Move the highlight bar to the desired number of lines on the display, using either the left- or right-arrow key. Press Enter to change the number of lines. Press Esc to leave without changing the number of lines on your computer screen. This option is only available on EGA and VGA-equipped computer systems.

F10 exits The Norton Change Directory. Pressing Esc is the same as using F10.

Norton Control Center

NCC

Purpose

Controls specific parts of your computer hardware, such as the computer keyboard, display, serial ports, and battery operated clocks. The following eight functions are available under The Norton Control Center:

Cursor Size	Sets cursor size.
DOS Color	Sets DOS colors.
Palette Colors	Sets palette colors.
Video Mode	Selects video mode.
Keyboard rate	Controls the rate and speed of keyboard repeat.
Serial Ports	Configures any serial port.
Watches	Sets one to four stopwatches.

Time and Date   Permanently changes the
                 system time and date on AT-
                 style computers.

Each option has its own detailed entry in this Quick
Reference.

Syntax

NCC [*filespec*][*switches*]

   or

NCC [*quick switches*]

   filespec   The name of the file in which
                       you previously saved the
                       settings using F2.

   switches/   The available switches
   quickswitches   you can use when starting The
                       Norton Control Center.

Switches

   /SETALL   Set all options saved in
                 filespec.

   /CURSOR   Set only the cursor size saved
                 in *filespec*.

   /KEYRATE   Set only the key rate saved in
                 filespec.

   /PALETTE   Set only the palette colors
                 saved in *filespec*.

   /COM*n*   Set only the serial port
                 numbered *n* saved in *filespec*.

   /DOSCOLOR   Set only the DOS colors saved
                 in *filespec*.

   /DISPLAY   Set only the display mode
                 saved in *filespec*.

Quick switches

/BW80	Set display mode to black and white, 25 by 80.
/C080	Set display mode to color, 25 by 80.
/25	Set display mode to 25 lines (same as /C080).
/35	Set display mode to 35 lines (EGA only).
/40	Set display mode to 40 lines (VGA only).
/43	Set display mode to 43 lines (EGA only).
/150	Set display mode to 50 lines (VGA only).
/FASTKEY	Set keyboard rate to fastest value.

Procedures

Note: Execute the following commands from the DOS prompt.

To access The Norton Control Center:

Type NCC and press Enter.

To change display settings:

To set a VGA screen to 40 lines, type NCC /40 and press Enter.

To set the computer's display to black and white, 25 by 80, type NCC /BW80 and press Enter.

To use other settings:

To use all the settings in the file SET, type NCC SET /SETALL and press Enter.

To use just the cursor setting in the file SET, type NCC SET /CURSOR and press Enter.

To use the keyrate and DOS Color setting in the file SET, type NCC SET /KEYRATE/DOSCOLOR and press Enter.

Notes

A summary of the NCC keys follows:

↑, ↓	Moves highlight to a different item in the function menu.
Enter **or** → Esc	Activates a function, exit function, and return to function menu. (If the highlight is already in the function menu, Esc quits NCC.)
Tab	Moves the highlight to the next field.
*	Resets the function to default settings.
F1	Gets context-sensitive help.
F2	Saves all changes to a designated file.
F10	Quits The Norton Control Center.

When you use F2 to create a file to hold your settings, the file can be used by Norton Control Center to restore your settings. The Norton Control Center prompts you via a dialog box to enter the name of a file to save the current settings. If you use this file the next time you run The Norton Control Center, the settings are made automatically for you.

Norton Disk Doctor

NDD

Purpose

Finds and corrects any physical or logical errors on floppy or hard disks.

Syntax

NDD [*d*:][*d*:][*switches*]

    d: The letter of the drive or drives you want to check.

    switches   The available switches you can use with Norton Disk Doctor.

Switches

    /QUICK   Omits test for bad data cylinders on the disk.

    /COMPLETE   Includes the tests for bad data cylinders.

Procedures

Note: Execute the following commands from the DOS prompt. Unless you specify the /QUICK or /COMPLETE switch as a part of your command line, NDD requires you to supply or verify certain information.

To run Norton Disk Doctor, type NDD and press Enter.

To run Norton Disk Doctor on drives C and D, type NDD C: D: and press Enter.

To run Norton Disk Doctor on drive A and to ignore the sector tests, type NDD A: /QUICK and press Enter.

To run Norton Disk Doctor on drives A and B, and test for all bad data sectors, type NDD A: B: /COMPLETE and press Enter.

Notes

The Norton Disk Doctor (NDD) runs many different tests. You can test more than one drive at a time by typing the drive letters, separated by a space. You can run NDD interactively or at the command line.

To run NDD at the command line, type the program name, one or more drive letters, and use the /Quick or /Complete switch. If you run NDD interactively, select Diagnose Disk to test the integrity of the disk, or select Common Solutions to review procedures you can follow to correct any damage.

Norton Integrator

NI

Purpose

Combines and organizes all The Norton Utilities. By using The Norton Integrator, you can highlight and run any one of The Norton Utilities.

Syntax

NI

Procedures

To start The Norton Integrator, from the DOS prompt, type NI and press Enter.

Press Esc or F10 to quit The Norton Integrator.

Notes

Use the up- or down-arrow key to move the highlight bar through the list of utilities. Help screens are displayed as each utility is highlighted. Type any parameters or switches, which appear on the bottom bar of the screen. Press Enter to run the utility.

Use any of these editing keys when working in The Norton Integrator:

→ or Ctrl-D	Move cursor right one character.
← or Ctrl-S	Move cursor left one character.
Ctrl-→ or Ctrl-F	Move cursor right one word.
Ctrl-← or Ctrl-A	Move cursor left one word.
Ctrl-Home	Move cursor to beginning of the line.
Ctrl-End	Move cursor to end of the line.
Backspace	Delete one character left of cursor.
Delete or Ctrl-G	Delete one character at the cursor.
Ctrl-T	Delete one word right of the cursor.
Ctrl-W	Delete one word left of the cursor.
Ctrl-Y	Delete the entire line.
Tab	Delete entire line, enter Speed Search.

After you run the utility, you return to The Norton Integrator.

The Norton Integrator keeps a history of the commands used. Press Ctrl-E to scroll backward through the list of commands or Ctrl-X to scroll forward.

Norton Utilities Main Program

NU

Purpose

Enables you to explore the disk and see and edit disk information in several formats, reports technical information about the disk and any files on the disk, searches for lost data, and recovers lost and erased files on the disk.

Caution: Be very careful when you explore, edit, and write to certain areas on your disk with this utility. Some of the areas of your computer system that you can explore and edit with The Norton Utilities Main Program are highly technical in nature. For example, if you make an error in writing to one of the DOS system areas on your disk, DOS may not be able to access your disk. Always back up the entire disk before editing.

The Norton Utilities documentation contains extensive, technical information about this utility. Use of The Norton Utilities Main Program by inexperienced or undertrained computer users can cause irreversible damage to data and files. This book is not intended as a replacement for the documentation that is included with your copy of Norton Utilities. Please refer to the documentation to obtain a complete discussion of The Norton Utilities Main Program.

The Norton Utilities Main Program provides access to the following menu options:

* Disk Information displays information about the disk and a map of disk usage.

* Explore Disk enables you to explore the disk and to display and edit disk information.

* Unerase recovers lost and erased files on disk.

Syntax

NU [*filespec*][*switches*]

    filespec   The specified files you want to examine.

switches	The available switches you can use with Norton Utilities.

Switches

/D*n*	Screen driver has two options. The default, *n*=0, is for IBM PCs and compatibles. Use *n*=1 with BIOS-compatible machines.
/BW (Alt-F1)	Enables the use of a monochrome composite monitor from a CGA card. You can access this within Norton Utilities also by pressing **Alt-F1**.
/EBCDIC (Alt-F5)	Interprets the characters in compliance with the EBCDIC encoding standard that is used on IBM mainframe computers. When in The Norton Utilities, press **Alt-F5** to toggle this option on and off.
/NOSNOW	Provides a cure to persistent, annoying screen flickers on older CGA display adapters.
/X:*drives*	Excludes the specified drives from an absolute sector processing. If you experience difficulty activating the absolute sector mode of Norton Utilities, this switch excludes allocated but non-existent drives from absolute sector processing. For example, use this switch to activate absolute sector processing in Zenith DOS.

Type **NU/X:DEF** to exclude drives D, E, and F, as Zenith DOS allocates these drives even if they do not exist on your computer.

/M   Places Norton Utilities into the maintenance mode and bypasses the DOS logical organization. You may need to use this switch if you are working with badly damaged disks.

/P(Alt-F2)   Displays only the printable characters and suppresses the IBM graphics characters on the screen. Use this switch to send a screen shot to your printer. You can also activate this option within Norton Utilities by pressing **Alt-F2**.

/WS(Alt-F6)   Turn on the WordStar mode (7 bits per character) or off (8 bits per character). When this switch is on, characters in the IBM PC extended character set do not display. You can also activate this option within Norton Utilities by pressing **Alt-F6**.

Procedure

To access The Norton Utilities main program, from the DOS prompt, type **NU** and press **Enter**.

Palette Colors

NCC

Purpose

Changes the palette colors. This option is available from the Norton Control Center on EGA and VGA equipped machines only.

Procedures

To use Palette Colors:

1. At the DOS prompt, type NCC and press Enter.

2. Select Palette Colors.

    The control area shows the current selection for each color in the palette. Although you can choose from 64 colors, the palette contains a total of 16 colors.

3. Use the up-arrow key, down-arrow key, or Tab to move the arrow highlight to the color you want to change.

4. Press + or - (on the numeric keyboard only) to change the highlighted color (+ increases the color number and - decreases it). Press the right-arrow to see a color menu.

5. Use either the left- or right-arrow key to make a new color selection and press Enter to accept the new color or Esc to leave the menu.

6. After you select the colors, press Enter to accept changes and return to the function menu. Or press Esc to return to the function menu and discard any changes made in the DOS color.

To restore default settings:

Press * (asterisk).

Note

Although your computer and programs use only 16 colors at a time, your computer can generate more than 16 colors. By using The Norton Control Center, you can decide what color to paste in any position.

Quick Unerase

Purpose

Recovers erased or deleted files quickly, using automatic features.

Syntax

QU [*filespec*][/A]

filespec	The specified files you want to examine.

Switch

/A	Unerases all files automatically.

Procedures

Note: Execute the following commands from the DOS prompt.

To unerase files in the current directory:

To unerase a file in the current directory, type QU and press **Enter**.

To unerase all files in the current directory, type QU /A and press **Enter**.

To unerase files in a specific directory:

To unerase all files in the Lotus directory, type QU \LOTUS*.* and press **Enter**.

To unerase files on a specific drive:

To unerase a file on drive A, type QU A:.

To unerase all files on drive A, type QU A: /A and
press Enter.

To unerase specific files:

To unerase the file REPORT.JAN in the current
directory, type QU REPORT.JAN and press Enter.

To unerase the file REPORT.JAN located in the
WP50 directory on drive C, type QU
C:\WP50\REPORT.JAN and press Enter.

Notes

Quick Unerase is an easy way to undelete an erased file.
When the program starts, it reports the number of files
that you can recover. You may not be able to recover all
the files because unerasing one file may increase the
chances of erasing another file.

If you have written to a disk since you erased the file,
you may find that you cannot recover the deleted file.

When a file is erased or deleted, DOS changes the first
letter of the file name to a ?. For example, a deleted file
originally called REPORT.JAN is listed as
?EPORT.JAN. During the Quick Unerase function, QU
asks for the missing first character of the file name.

If you use the /A switch to unerase files, Quick Unerase
automatically fills in the missing character of the file
name, using a unique first letter of the alphabet. To
rename the file, use the DOS REName command to give
the file the name you desire.

If a file cannot be unerased, QU advises you.

Safe Format

SF

Purpose

Offers a safe, fast, easy alternative to the DOS
FORMAT command. Makes it easier to recover from an
accidental formatting of a disk.

Syntax

SF [*d*:][*switches*]

or

FORMAT [*d*:][*switches*]

Note: FORMAT works only if you selected this option during The Norton Utilities Installation program.

d:	The letter of the drive you want to format.
filespec	The specified files you want to examine.

Switches

/A	Run Safe format in the Automatic mode. (This switch is useful in batch files.)
/S	Copy the system files to a disk so that the disk is a system disk.
/B	Leave space for system files.
/V:*label*	Place volume label with text label on disk.
/1	Format single-sided disk.
/4	Format 360K diskette in 1.2M drive.
/8	Format 8 sectors per track.
/N:*n*	Number of sectors per track (n=8, 9, 15, or 18).
/T:*n*	Number of tracks (n=40 or 80).
/*size*	Size of diskette.
/Q	Use Quick Format.
/D	Use DOS Format.
/C	Use Complete Format (diskettes only).

Procedure

To start Safe Format, from the DOS prompt, type SF and then press Enter.

Notes

If you used the installation program included with The Norton Utilities, the DOS FORMAT program was renamed, and each time you type FORMAT the Safe Format screen appears.

If you start Safe Format without a drive specified, you must select the disk drive you want to format.

The Safe Format screen is divided into two main areas. Information about the formatting yet to be done, current status, and information about the disk being formatted are shown on the right side of the screen. On the left side, helpful information is provided. The following section discusses this information.

Using the installation program, you can substitute Safe Format for the regular DOS FORMAT command. In the process, DOS FORMAT is renamed to XXFORMAT. Then, whenever you enter FORMAT, the following options appear:

To Begin Format, press Enter. If the disk contains data, you are asked if you want to proceed. This prompt enables you to remove important disks before formatting and losing data.

Drive displays a dialog box in which you select the drive you want to format. To select a drive within this dialog box, use the left- or right-arrow key to move the highlight to the drive you want to format and press Enter. Or, type the drive letter. The current drive is shown at the bottom of the dialog box. Press Esc to exit the dialog box without making changes.

Size displays a dialog box in which you select how much data a floppy disk can store. Use the left- or right-arrow key to move through the range of

choices to highlight the desired size and press
Enter. Esc exits without changing the current size
setting, which is shown in the bottom of the dialog
box.

Note: You cannot use Size to change the physical
size of a hard disk partition. To change the size of a
hard disk, use DOS's FDISK command. If you
attempt to change the size of a hard disk, a dialog
box appears and advises you that the procedure
cannot be done. Press Enter or Esc to dismiss the
dialog box.

System Type displays a dialog box to select whether
to install the DOS system files on the newly
formatted disk. You also can choose to reserve
space for the DOS system files at a later date
without actually installing them now. Use the
cursor-movement keys to choose the option you
want and press Enter. Press Esc to leave the dialog
box without making changes.

Volume Label enables you to enter up to an 11-
character name for the disk you want to format.
Type the name and press Enter. Press Esc to
dismiss the dialog box without changing the current
volume label setting.

Format Mode displays a dialog box to set the type of
format. Use the cursor-movement keys to move the
highlight to your choice and press Enter. You have
the following four choices available in Format
Mode:

- Safe Format uses The Norton Utilities
  formatting algorithm. It does not erase all data
  on a disk. Because the information is still on
  the disk, both Quick UnErase and Unremove
  Directory can recover your data after a Safe
  Format, which they cannot do if you use the
  Format command supplied with DOS. This
  mode is also much faster than DOS FORMAT.

- Quick Format delivers a faster formatting procedure by placing a new system area on the disk. It is used to erase a floppy disk without reformatting to remove a large directory tree from a hard disk. This format mode is complete within just a few seconds.

- DOS Format uses the regular DOS formatting procedure. All data on the floppy disk is erased.

- Complete Format works like Safe Format, except that bad sectors are reformatted to make the disk more reliable. This mode is not available on hard disks.

- Quit exits Safe Format.

When formatting is complete, a dialog box appears. Press either Enter or Esc to dismiss the dialog box.

Before formatting a disk, Safe Format analyzes the disk and saves the information it gathers in a special file so that the disk can be reconstructed even after formatting is complete. UnErase was enhanced to take advantage of this feature.

If a disk is accidentally formatted using Safe Format, you can use the RESTORE option with Format Recover to fully recover your data.

Serial Ports

NCC

Purpose

Configures the serial ports on your computer.

Procedures

To configure the serial ports on your computer:

1. At the DOS prompt, type NCC and press Enter.
2. Select Serial Ports.

The control area then shows your computer's serial ports and the settings available. The current setting for each parameter is marked by a check mark.

3. Use the up- or down-arrow key to select the port you want to configure first.

   The port currently being configured has a check mark in the Port column. A summary of the current settings for the serial port is displayed at the bottom of your screen.

4. Use either the left- or right-arrow key to move from parameter to parameter (such as to move from port to baud rate to parity).

5. Use the up- and down-arrow key to change the setting of the selected parameter.

6. Press **Enter** to accept the changes you make to the serial port settings and to exit. Or press **Esc** from within the Serial Ports window to discard any changes made to the serial port and return to the function menu.

For each serial port on your computer, you can change these parameters:

Baud	The speed of the communications to take place. Common settings for communications by modem are 300, 1200, and 2400. Serial printers are often set at either 4800 or 9600.
Parity	The type of error-checking convention to use. "None" is the common choice in most serial communication settings.
Databits	The total number of data bits sent with each pulse of information.
Stopbits	The total number of stop bits (a signal that this individual pulse is finished) that is sent with each pulse of information.

To restore the default settings of the serial ports:
Press * from within the Serial Ports window.

Speed Disk

SD

Purpose

Speeds up your disk by eliminating file fragmentation and by reorganizing the directory and file placement. By eliminating excessive movement of the read-write head in your disk drive, the speed of your disk is increased. Speed Disk can also generate a report on the fragmentation of your files on a disk.

Syntax

SD [*d*:][*switches*]

or

SD [*item to report on*][*switches*]

d:	The letter of the drive you want to use Speed Disk.
switches	The available switches you can use with Speed Disk.

Switches

/C	Complete Optimization of the disk.
/D	Directory Optimization.
/P	Pauses the display after each full screen. (Pressing any key also pauses the display.)
/Q	Quick compress optimization.
/REPORT	Generates a fragmentation report, but does not rearrange the disk.
/S	Reports on the files in subdirectories.

/T   Shows the totals only.

/U   Unfragments files optimization.

Procedures

Note: Executing this utility from the DOS prompt automatically puts you in the interactive mode. Utilizing the available switches eliminates the need for an excessive selection process. For example, SD A: /Q tells Speed Disk that you want a QUICK operation on drive A. The status area of your screen indicates this, and all that remains is to tell Speed Disk to optimize the drive.

To run Speed Disk:

To run Speed Disk on drive C:

1. Type SD and press Enter.

2. Select drive C.

3. Select Optimize Disk.

To run Speed Disk on drive C and perform complete optimization of the disk, type SD C: /C and press Enter.

To run Speed Disk on drive C and to complete only a quick compress optimization, type SD C: /Q and press Enter.

To run Speed Disk on drive A, type SD A: and press Enter.

To run Speed Disk in batch mode, follow the program name with the drive letter you want to optimize, plus any switch. You can specify any of the sort methods available in interactive mode using the switches /C for Complete, /D for Directory only, /Q for Quick Compress, and /U for Unfragment only.

To generate a report:

To run a report on the fragmentation of the disk in drive A, type SD A: /REPORT and press Enter.

To generate a report on only the files in the \DOS directory on the current drive, type SD \DOS /S/ REPORT and press Enter.

Options

These options are available to set the way Speed Disk optimizes your disk:

- Optimize Disk begins optimizing the disk according to the currently-selected options.

- Change Drive changes the current drive.

- Set Options customizes the layout of files and directories on your disk to provide maximum performance for your particular work style. Enables you to specify the placement of directories, files to be moved to the front of the disk, files you do not want moved, and the type of sorting you want performed.

  All options are saved in the file SD.INI on your root directory. The next time you run Speed Disk, the options are automatically set as your default options.

- Directory Order specifies the sort order of directories on the disk. The specified directory order appears in a window on the right side of the screen. All directories that appear in this window are placed at the beginning of the disk, minimizing their access time. The default order is the current path. A directory tree appears in a window on the left side of the screen. Press Tab to move between the two windows.

  To add a directory, press Tab to move the highlight to the Tree window. Highlight the directory you want to add by using either speed search or the up- or down-arrow key; then press Enter. The directory is added to the end of the directory list in the right window.

  To move a directory, make sure that the highlight is in the right directory sort window, use the left- or right-arrow key to select Move, and press Enter.

Use the up- or down-arrow key to move the selected directory up and down in the list. Finally, store the directory at the desired location by pressing Enter.

Delete a directory from the list by using the up- and down-arrow keys to highlight it. Then use the left- or right-arrow key to select Delete and press Enter.

When the directory is arranged to your satisfaction, return to the main screen by highlighting Done and pressing Enter.

• Files to Put First moves selected files to the front of the disk. An empty box appears. Type the name of the file and press Enter. Another box for the next file name appears. Make sure that the cursor is in an empty box and press Enter when you finish. This option is particularly useful with wild cards. Type

    *.EXE
    *.COM

to move all executable files to the front of the disk.

• Unmovable Files—All hidden files are considered unmovable by Speed Disk. Add and delete files from this list using the preceding techniques.

• Optimization Method—Speed Disk provides four different techniques for optimizing your disk that range from a complete, but lengthy full optimization, to a quick compression.

    Complete Optimization
    File Unfragment
    Only Optimize Directories
    Quick Compress

Complete Optimization is the most complete method of optimizing the disk. This option offers the greatest improvements in disk speed, and takes the longest to run. In this option, all specified directories are moved toward the front of the disk, as are any specified files. Then all other files are unfragmented as data is compressed and moved forward. When this optimization is finished, there are no "holes" in the disk structure.

File Unfragment is faster than full optimization. Attempts to defragment as many files as possible. It does not necessarily fill in all the holes in the disk, and some large files may not be unfragmented at all.

Only Optimize Directories—The only data moved in this method is directories. Files are not unfragmented, and holes can remain in the disk structure. Nonetheless, optimizing the directory layout can significantly improve the disk speed.

Quick Compress moves data forward on the disk to fill in any free space. It does not unfragment files. This method is fast, but may or may not affect significant speed improvements. Any new files added to the disk go at the end of the disk and are unfragmented.

- Verify On/Off—Turn on verify to have data that is written read back immediately to confirm accurate operation. By default, this option is off.

- Disk Statistics reports on a number of optimization-related disk parameters.

- Exit Speed Disk enables you to leave Speed Disk and return to DOS.

Notes

Before running Speed Disk, deactivate any memory-resident programs.

You can run Speed Disk from the DOS command line or interactively. If you run Speed Disk from the DOS command line, you return to the DOS command line when optimization is complete.

Caution: Do not turn off your computer when Speed Disk is running. Doing so can damage your files. To interrupt Speed Disk, press **Esc**.

To assist you in determining whether you need to run Speed Disk, you can generate a fragmentation report by specifying the /REPORT switch. When you use the /REPORT switch, SD generates a report, but does not rearrange the disk. You can ask for a report on the whole drive, a directory, or a file. A report of 100 percent indicates no fragmentation has occurred on your disk.

Some copy-protected programs place one or more files on your hard disk that must not be relocated. These programs make note of the original location of the files. If the files are moved, the copy protection scheme assumes that an illegal copy was made and prevents the program from running.

Most of these protection techniques set the hidden, or system, attribute for their immovable files. Some copy-protected programs use other methods. Speed Disk uses special precautions to avoid disturbing such programs. Each file on the disk is examined separately. Any hidden file or hidden subdirectory, any files within a hidden subdirectory, and any subdirectories of hidden subdirectories are never moved by Speed Disk.

Copy-protection schemes, such as from Vault and Softguard Systems, do not hide their copy-protected program files. Speed Disk recognizes these files as well, and does not move them. You can override this option and move these files by explicitly deleting them from the list of Unmovable Files. Use the Unmovable Files option in the Set Sort Options menu.

System Information

SI

Purpose

Runs tests on your computer, determines the configuration of your computer, and reports results of its findings to you.

Syntax

SI [*d:*][*switches*]

d:	The letter of the drive you want to test. (With System Information, you can test only hard drives, not floppy disk drives.)
switches	The available switches you can use with System Information.

Switches

/A	ANSI mode only. System Information skips the BIOS- specific features.
/N	Skips the live memory probe. (On some computers, a live memory probe requires a reboot.
/LOG	Prepares a report in a format for printing or sending to a file.

Procedures

Note: Execute the following commands from the DOS prompt.

To check the System Information on the current drive, type SI and press Enter.

To check the System Information on drive D, type SI D: and press Enter.

To check the System Information on drive D in ANSI mode only, type SI /A and press Enter.

To check the System Information on the current drive and skip the live memory probe, type SI /N and press Enter.

To check the System Information on the current drive and to prepare a report, type SI /LOG and press Enter.

Notes

System Information provides a report about your computer. System Information issues two separate memory reports. One report is based on information supplied by DOS, and shows the total amount of

memory, the amount reserved by DOS and resident
programs, and the amount of memory available for your
application programs. The second report is based on a
live test, and is performed by probing every part of
computer memory.

Note: When System Information attempts to probe
nonexistent memory, your computer may lock up and
report a parity error. Although this error does not harm
the computer, it does require you to reboot the computer.
The /N (No memory test) switch bypasses this test.

The memory test reports four categories of memory—
amount of main memory as reported by DOS (usually
equal to the total amount of main memory), memory
used by screen display adapters, expanded and extended
memory, and memory used by ROM-BIOS extensions.

System Information attempts to identify and report the
type of computer running the main microprocessor, the
DOS version running, and the BIOS date. All the
standard IBM PC family members are recognized.
System Information also recognizes specialty models of
the PC family, such as the 3270-PC, and many of the PC
compatibles, but it cannot identify all the MS-DOS
computers in existence. If System Information does not
recognize your machine, it attempts to find and show
identifying marks, such as a copyright notice in the
computer's ROM-BIOS.

System Information determines and reports the
equipment attached to the computer, including
coprocessors, parallel and serial ports, video display
adapter(s) and current video mode, and number of
logical disk drives.

Add-in boards in some computers have on-board ROMs
that control the operation of equipment on (or attached
to) the boards. These ROMS are "mapped" into the
computer's memory space and are reported by System
Information as "ROM-BIOS extensions." If you use a
computer with a hard disk, you may see a ROM-BIOS
extension reported at address C800 (the standard address
for the hard disk control ROM).

System Information measures two aspects of your
computer's performance—processor performance,
reported as CI (Computing Index), and disk
performance, reported as DI (Disk Index). These two
indexes are weighted and combined to generate the
indicator of overall system performance, PI
(Performance Index).

The indexes are calculated relative to the performance of
an original IBM PC-XT. A CI of 2.5 means that the
processor in your computer is two-and-a-half times
faster than that of a standard XT.

Note: You may receive an invalid error message when
you run System Information without switches. If you
receive an error message, rerun System Information with
the /A (ANSI) switch.

Text Search

TS

Purpose

Searches for text or data in one or multiple files, across
an entire disk or across the erased file space of an entire
disk.

Syntax

For searching files:

TS [*filespec*][*search-text*][/S][/T][*common-
switches*]

filespec	Specifies the file to be searched.
search-text	The text to search for. Place quotation marks around any text that contains embedded spaces.

For searching the entire disk:

TS [*search-text*] /D [*common-switches*]

For searching the erased file space:

TS [*search-text*] /E [*common-switches*]

Switches

/A	Automates the text search by automatically answering yes to the Search for more data? prompt.
/CS	Causes the search to be case sensitive.
/EBCDIC	Specifies the files being searched are encoded in the EBCDIC file format.
/LOG	Prepares a report in a format for printing or saving as a file.
/WS	Does not consider characters in the IBM PC extended character set in the search. By default, Text Search looks for extended characters.

For searching files:

/S	Includes subdirectories in the search.
/T	Sets noninteractive summary total mode.

For searching erased file space:

/D	Searches the entire disk.
/E	Searches the erased data space of the entire disk.
/Cn	Begins the search at cluster *n*.

Procedures

Note: Execute the following commands from the DOS prompt.

To run Text Search interactively:

1. Type **TS** and press **Enter**.
2. Choose whether you want to search **F**iles, **D**isk, or **E**rased File.
3. Type the drive you want to search.

4. If you want to copy the text to a file, enter the file name and press Enter. If you don't want to copy the text to a file, just press Enter.

5. Type the text you want to search and press Enter.

TS reports where it finds the text string.

To perform special searches:

To search for the word "December" on all .RPT file, type **TS *.RPT "December" /S** and press Enter.

To search the entire disk for the word "December", type **TS "December" /D** and press Enter.

To search for the word "December" in an erased file, type **TS "December" /E** and press Enter.

Notes

The filespec can include the DOS wild card characters * and ?.

Use the /S switch to search the entire disk, including all subdirectories. Unless you use the /CS switch, Text Search is case sensitive.

Time and Date

NCC

Purpose

Sets the DOS system time and date within the Norton Control Center.

Procedures

1. At the DOS prompt, type **NCC** and press Enter.

2. Select Time and Date.

3. Use the up- or down-arrow keys or the Tab key to select either Time or Date.

The setting you select appears in inverse video.

4. Use the left- or right-arrow keys to select any part of the time or date you want to set (month, date, year for the date; hours, minutes, seconds).

5. Use the + and - keys on the numeric keypad to increase or decrease the selected number. You also can type the desired value.

6. Press **Enter** to make changes to the DOS time and date and exit. Press **Esc** to exit without changing the DOS time and date.

Time Mark

TM

Purpose

Displays the date and time in a more legible format than DOS. Acts as a stopwatch to time up to four different durations of your various computer operations.

Syntax

TM [START][STOP][*comment*][*switches*]

START	Resets the stopwatch and displays the current time and date.
STOP	Displays the interval since the last start, and does *not* reset the stopwatch.
comment	Displays the text when the command is executed. Used when you run multiple timers via batch files.
switches	The available switches you can use with Time Mark.

Switches

/C*n*	Selects one of four independent counters or stopwatches numbered 1 to 4. If you specify none, Time Mark uses C1.

/L   Places Time Mark information on the
                    left side of the screen. When this
                    switch is not used, Time Mark places
                    the information on the right side of
                    the screen.

/LOG   Formats the output for printing to a
                    disk file.

/N   Does not show the current time and
                    date display; shows the elapsed time
                    intervals only.

Procedures

Note: Execute the following commands from the DOS
prompt.

To check the current time and date, type TM and press
Enter.

To start timing an interval, type TM START and press
Enter.

To stop timing an interval, type TM STOP and press
Enter.

To start a second, separate stopwatch, type TM START
/C2 and press Enter.

To stop the second stopwatch and display the comment,
Time logged onto Compuserve, type TM
STOP "Time logged onto Compuserve" /C2 and press
Enter.

To start timing a third interval, and append the output to
a file called TIME.LOG, type TM START /C3/
LOG>>WORK.LOG and press Enter.

Notes

Time Mark displays the current date, time, and elapsed
time as

```
10:21 am, Friday, August 18, 1989

4 hours, 43 minutes, 3 seconds
```

The elapsed time, which appears on the second line,
appears only when Time Mark is used with the STOP

parameter. Without the STOP parameter, Time Mark displays only the current date and time on the first line.

If a comment includes any spaces, be sure that you enclose the comment within quotation marks.

UnErase

NU

Purpose

Recovers lost and erased files on disk.

Procedures

1. Select Unerase. The Recover Erased File menu appears.

2. Select Change drive or directory if you need to change the drive or directory; then select the drive or directory on which the file is located. If you elect to change the drive or directory, you must select Return to Recover erase file from the Change Drive or Directory menu.

3. Choose Select Erased File.

4. Move the highlight bar to the desired file and press Enter.

5. Type the first letter of the file name and press Enter.

6. Choose UnErase menu.

7. Tab to All Clusters Automatically and press Enter.

8. Select Save Erased Files.

Unremove Directory

UD

Purpose

Recovers removed directories and the catalog of erased files contained within the removed directories.

Syntax

UD [*directory pathname*]

Procedures

Note: Execute the following commands from the DOS prompt.

To unremove a directory from the current drive, type UD and press Enter.

To unremove a directory from drive A, type UD A: and press Enter.

To unremove the directory \REPORTS from the current drive, type UD \REPORTS and press Enter.

Notes

If the directory name you want unremoved is not listed in the command, UD asks for the name of the directory.

UD performs two functions. First, it unremoves a directory that you removed by using the DOS RMDIR or RD command. Then UD searches for groups of files that were in the directory. You can accept or reject each group of files UD finds. To recover the files, use Quick Unerase.

Video Mode

NCC

Purpose

Changes the video mode of your computer.

Procedures

1. At the DOS prompt, type **NCC** and press **Enter**.

2. Select Video Mode.

   The control area changes to show the different video modes available. A check mark appears next to the current video option.

3. Use the up- or down-arrow keys or **Tab** to select the video mode you want.

4. Press **Enter** to activate the selected video mode and to return to the function menu.

   To restore the default video mode selection, press *.

Note

If you set the video mode to black-and-white, you cannot select any palette colors.

Volume Label

VL

Purpose

Views, adds, changes, or deletes an electronic disk label.

Syntax

VL [*d:*] [*label*]

d:	The letter of the drive you want to label.
label	The label you want to add.

Procedures

Note: Execute the following commands from the DOS prompt.

To view a volume label:

To view the Volume (electronic disk) label on the current drive, type **VL** and press **Enter**.

To delete a volume label:

To delete the volume label on the current drive, do the following:

1. Type **VL** and press **Enter**.

2. Press **Delete**.

To add a volume label:

To add a Volume (electronic disk) label to drive C called Fixed-Disk, type **VL C: Fixed-Disk** and press **Enter**.

Note

If you want to use spaces within the volume label, you must include the label in quotation marks.

Watches

NCC

Purpose

Keeps track of time like an electronic stopwatch. When a timer is started, the start time is recorded. The timer tracks elapsed time to one-tenth of a second.

Procedures

1. At the DOS prompt, type **NCC** and press **Enter**.

2. Select Watches from the Norton Control Center main menu.

3. Use either the up- or down-arrow key to select one of the four timers.

4. Use either the right- or left-arrow key to select either Start/Pause or Reset Clock.

5. Press **Enter**. Press **Esc** to exit.

Notes

When using a watch in The Norton Control Center, pressing Esc does not discard settings. Rather, you must reset each watch specifically. Typing an asterisk does not restore any previous timer settings.

The Watches function in the Norton Control Center is fully compatible with the Time Mark program.

Wipedisk

WIPEDISK

Purpose

Overwrites, erases, and wipes clean every portion of a disk. Replaces all information on the disk with zeros so that you can wipe clean a disk containing confidential information. After running Wipedisk, any confidential data on the disk is destroyed.

Caution: Become familiar with the WIPEDISK and WIPEFILE commands. The purpose of these two utilities is to destroy the selected disk or files. Norton's UNERASE command is not capable of restoring wiped files.

Syntax

WIPEDISK [*d:*][*switches*]

d:	The letter of the drive you want to wipe clean.
switches	The available switches you can use with Wipedisk.

Switches

/E	Specifies that erased or unused data space is wiped. This switch saves current data, but wipes erased data.
/G*n*	Follows certain government rules for security wiping. *n* specifies the

number of times the wiping pattern is repeated. The standard default is 3.

/LOG   Prepares a report in a format for printing or sending to a file.

/R*n*   Sets repeated wiping. *n* sets the number of times the data is overwritten.

/V*n*   Sets the value used to overwrite the disk. *n* can be any number from 0 to 255. The default is 0, unless the /G switch is used. If /G is used, the default for the /V switch is changed to 246 (F6, hexadecimal).

Procedures

Note: Execute the following commands from the DOS prompt.

To use Wipedisk on drive A, type WIPEDISK A: and press Enter.

To wipe only the erased data space of drive A, type WIPEDISK A: /E and press Enter.

To wipe the disk in drive A four times with the value of 100, type WIPEDISK A: /R4/V100 and press Enter.

Notes

The program asks for confirmation before beginning to wipe your disk. Type Y to proceed with wiping the entire disk.

The Norton Utilities UNERASE program cannot recover files Wipedisk obliterates.

Wipefile

WIPEFILE

Purpose

Protects confidential data by overwriting or obliterating files.

Syntax

WIPEFILE [*filespec*][*switches*]

filespec	The file or files to wipe.
switches	The available switches you can use with Wipefile.

Switches

/G*n*	Follows certain government rules for security wiping. *n* specifies the number of times the wiping pattern repeats. The standard default is 3.
/LOG	Prepares a report in a format for printing or sending to a file.
/N	Places Wipefile in a non-wiping mode. Erases or deletes the file, but does not wipe it. (This is similar to the DOS DEL command.)
/P	Pauses for confirmation before actually deleting and wiping each file.
/R*n*	Sets repeated wiping. *n* sets the number of times the data is overwritten.
/S	Wipes (or deletes, if the /N switch is used) all files in the subdirectories.
/V*n*	Sets the value used to overwrite the disk. *n* can be any number from 0 to 255. The default is 0, unless the /G switch is used. If /G is used, the default for the /V switch is changed to 246 (F6, hexadecimal).

Procedures

Note: Execute the following commands from the DOS prompt.

To wipe a particular file:

To wipe the file MARCH.RPT on the current drive, type **WIPEFILE MARCH.RPT** and press **Enter**.

To wipe the file MARCH.RPT on drive A, type
WIPEFILE A:MARCH.RPT and press Enter.

To wipe the file MARCH.RPT from the REPORTS
directory from the current drive, type WIPEFILE
\REPORTS\MARCH.RPT and press Enter.

To wipe a particular group of files:

To wipe all files on the current drive with the
extension .RPT, type WIPEFILE *.RPT and press
Enter.

To wipe all files on the current drive with the
extension .RPT, and pause for confirmation before
wiping, type WIPEFILE *.RPT /P and press
Enter.

To wipe all files on a particular drive:

To wipe all files on drive B, type WIPEFILE B:*.*
/S and press Enter.

To wipe all files on drive B, and pause for
confirmation before wiping, type WIPEFILE B:*.*
/S/P and press Enter.

Notes

You can include a drive, path name, and the DOS wild
card characters * or ? with Wipefile. You must specify a
file or files before Wipefile runs.

Wipefile can find and wipe hidden, system, and read-
only files. Wipefile always pauses and awaits
confirmation before wiping any of the files with these
attributes.

When a file is erased with the DOS DEL command, the
data is not actually erased. DOS marks the files as
erased, and the file's data space is marked as being
available, but the data is still intact. The only way to
erase the data is to overwrite it. Wipefile writes 0's on
the disk, unless you set a different value with the /V
switch.

NORTON COMMANDER

Controlling DOS and handling DOS commands is easy
when you use The Norton Commander. After you
master the commands, you can change, move, or delete
directories; view your dBASE or Lotus files; quickly
find files; and inspect, edit, copy, rename, move, or
delete any regular DOS file.

The Norton Commander includes several files. Only
four files are included with your original copy of the
program. The others are created by The Norton
Commander, which customizes the program to each
computer and the programs being used on it.

The Norton Commander program consists of these files:

    NC.EXE
    NCSMALL.EXE
    DBVIEW.EXE
    123VIEW.EXE

The Norton Commander creates the following files to
work with your computer and its installed applications:

    NC.EXT
    NC.INI
    NC.MNU
    TREEINFO.NCD
    DIRINFO

Always keep these files in the NC directory, which was
created during installation.

Starting The Commander

Because The Norton Commander is not a memory-
resident program, it does not interfere with any of your
memory-resident software you use. Always load any
memory-resident software before you start The Norton
Commander.

Procedure

From the DOS prompt, type NC and press Enter.

Notes

If you are using a computer with a hard disk, you can free some of your computer's memory by using the command NCSMALL. This command installs a reloader program that swaps The Norton Commander in and out of your computer system's memory, which provides more memory to run other programs.

Because access time is too slow, it is not recommended that you use NCSMALL on a two-floppy disk computer system.

You can have NC or NCSMALL come up automatically each time you start your computer by editing your AUTOEXEC.BAT file. By adding either NC or NCSMALL after the path statement in your AUTOEXEC.BAT file, The Norton Commander automatically loads each time you start your computer.

The Commander Screen

The Norton Commander screen contains four main sections and features. The main sections are the menu bar, panels, the DOS command line, and the function key bar.

The menu bar, if active, appears at the top of the computer screen. (To activate the menu bar, press F9.) The Norton Commander panels appear in the panel area, located in the main section of the screen. The DOS command line appears in the lower left of your screen when The Norton Commander is being used. The function key bar is always located at the bottom of the computer screen, and any function key displayed can be activated to select an option.

The Norton Commander contains left and right panels. When you first start The Norton Commander, only the right panel is displayed. The left panel is turned off.

Each panel can display a directory, subdirectory listing, or a directory tree. The Norton Commander also displays information about your computer system in the panels.

Only one panel is active at a time. If both panels are displayed, the title bar of the active panel is displayed in reverse video. Most operations of The Norton Commander are confined to the active panel, although some of the commands use the inactive panel as the target. For example, with the Copy command, The Norton Commander can send a copy of any specified file from the active panel to the inactive panel.

You can choose to display panels together or individually. To do so, use these commands:

Ctrl-P   Displays or does not display the active panel.

Ctrl-O   Displays or does not display both panels.

If both panels are displayed, press Tab to switch between the left and right panel to make one or the other active. If you are using a mouse, simply move the mouse to the desired panel and click the left mouse button to make the panel active.

When the active panel is set to display a file listing, all the files and subdirectories on the drive are displayed. Hidden files, those files which the attributes are set to hide the file during the DIR command, are also displayed. Hidden files are displayed with a grey-colored rectangle before the file extension.

You can copy, delete, move, or rename files or directories in the active panel. You also can change directories or load files into their applications.

You can move the *File Selection Bar*, a line located within the active directory panel, by using the up arrow, down arrow, Home, End, PgUp, or PgDn keys. You also can move the bar with your mouse. The File Selection Bar is used to mark or highlight files or directories.

Within the File Panel, you can change a directory by moving the File Selection Bar to the desired directory and then pressing Enter. The file listing changes to display the contents of the selected directory.

To move up a level in the directory structure, move the File Selection Bar to the line with the double dots . ., which is always located at the top of the listing. After positioning the File Selection Bar over the . . , press Enter.

Press Ctrl-PgUp to move back to the parent directory. To move to the root directory, press Ctrl-\.

If your computer is equipped with a mouse, you can change directories by positioning the mouse cursor over the directory's name, and double clicking the left mouse button. Move the mouse cursor to the . . and double click the left mouse button to move up a level in the directory structure.

To rapidly locate a file or directory within the File Panel, press and hold Alt, and then type the name of the file or directory you want to locate. The File Selection Bar moves to the first file or directory that is a possible match. Press Ctrl-Enter to move to the next potential match. During typing, a small dialog box appears to display the file name or directory you type. To dismiss this dialog box, press Esc.

You may want to have more than one file marked. To do so, move the File Selection Bar to the first file you want marked and press Insert. The file appears highlighted. Move the File Selection Bar to the next desired file and press Insert. You can mark as many multiple files as desired. To unmark a marked file, move the File Selection Bar to the highlighted, marked file and press Insert.

If your computer is equipped with a mouse, you can mark multiple files by moving the mouse cursor to the desired file and clicking the right mouse button. You can unmark files by moving the mouse cursor to the marked file and clicking the right mouse button.

The + and - keys (located on the numeric keyboard) can be used to call up a dialog box. The + marks files, and the - unmarks files. After this dialog box appears, you can type in any file specification. You can use the standard DOS wild cards * and ? to specify files. For example, to mark all files in the File Panel that have an extension of .TXT, press +, type *.TXT, and then press Enter.

You also can use the + and - keys to select all files except those specified. For example, to mark all files in the directory except those that have an extension of .TXT, press +, press **Enter**, press -, type *.TXT, and press **Enter**.

As files are marked, a running total of the file sizes and number of marked files are displayed on a status line.

The Tree Panels show a graphical listing of the directories on the current drive. You then can scroll through the directories listed or search for a specific directory.

The current directory always appears in bold on the graphic tree. A left arrow appears on the side of the panel to indicate the selected line.

You can use the Tree Panel to select a directory. Move the File Selection Bar by pressing the up arrow, down arrow, Home, End, PgUp, or PgDn keys. Then press **Enter** to move to the directory, and to make it the current directory. If two panels are displayed, the second one shows the contents of the new directory.

The Alt key works just as it does in the File Panel to search for a specific directory. Press + and - sign on the numeric keypad to move up or down the listing.

If your computer is equipped with a mouse, you can use the mouse to select a directory in the tree panel. Move the mouse cursor to the desired directory and click the left mouse button once to move the File Selection Bar to that directory. Click the left mouse button twice to move the File Selection Bar and to change the default directory.

The Norton Commander can supply information about your computer system. This information includes the total amount of memory available on your computer, the capacity of your drive, the amount of free space, the amount of free memory, and information about the current directory. The information is displayed in an info panel.

If the active panel is an info panel, pressing **Ctrl-L** changes the panel back to a directory or a tree panel. If the active panel is a directory or tree panel, pressing **Ctrl-L** switches the panel to an Info Display panel.

Dirinfo is a text file that is available for you to add information. You can add notes about your directories. To edit the Dirinfo file, press F4.

Commander Keys

You can use the following edit and cursor-movement keys in The Norton Commander:

Command Line Keys

Enter	Starts the DOS command.
Ctrl-Enter	Copies the name to the command line or command completion.
Ctrl-→ or Ctrl-F	Moves word right.
Ctrl-← or Ctrl-A	Moves word left.
Ctrl-Backspace or Ctrl-W	Deletes word left.
Ctrl-T	Deletes word right.
Ctrl-K	Deletes to the end of the line.
Ctrl-Y or Esc	Deletes the line.
Ctrl-G or Del	Deletes the character under the cursor.
Backspace	Deletes the character left of the cursor.
Ctrl-E	Recalls the previous command in history.
↑	Recalls the previous command in history, when both panels are off.

Ctrl-X	Recalls the next command in history.
↓	Recalls the next command in history, when both panels are off.
Ctrl-S	Moves cursor left one character.
←	Moves cursor left one character, except when a brief panel is active.
→	Moves cursor right one character, except when a brief panel is active.
Ctrl-D	Moves cursor right one character.

Panel Keys

↑	Moves cursor up one file in a directory.
↓	Moves cursor down one file in a directory.
←	Moves cursor left in Brief mode.
→	Moves cursor right in Brief mode.
PgUp	Pages up in the directory.
PgDn	Pages down in the directory.
Home	Moves to the first file in the directory.
End	Moves to the last file in the directory.

Ctrl-R	Selects a drive to view in the active panel, and re-reads the directory.
Ctrl-Enter	Copies files or directory names to the DOS command line or command completion.
Tab	Switches panels.
Ctrl-P	Toggles inactive panel on and off.
Ctrl-L	Toggles status panel.
Ctrl-O	Toggles panels on and off.
Ctrl-U	Swaps the panels.

File Panel Keys

Enter	Points and shoots.
Ctrl-PgUp	Changes to the parent directory (similar to the DOS command, CD..).
Ctrl-\	Changes to the root directory (similar to the DOS command, CD\ ).
+	Selects multiple files.
-	Unselects a group of files.
Alt-	Searches for typed text.
Insert	Selects, unselects file under the cursor.
Ctrl-Enter	Copies file or directory name to the DOS Command Line or command completion.

Tree Panel Keys

Enter	Changes to the directory under the cursor.
+	Moves down at the same level.
-	Moves up at the same level.
Alt-	Searches for typed text.

Info Panel Keys

Ctrl-L	Switches between status panel.
F4	Edits the file dirinfo.

Edit Keys

Backspace	Deletes character left.
Ctrl-A	Moves word left.
Ctrl-Backspace	Deletes word left.
Ctrl-C	Moves page down.
Ctrl-D	Moves cursor right.
Ctrl-E	Moves cursor up one line.
Ctrl-End	Moves to end of a file.
Ctrl-F	Moves word right.
Ctrl-G	Deletes character under cursor.
Ctrl-Home	Moves to start of a file.
Ctrl-K	Deletes to end of line.
Ctrl-←	Moves word right.
Ctrl-PgDn	Moves to end of a file.
Ctrl-PgUp	Moves to start of a file.
Ctrl-Q	Quotes next character.

Ctrl-R	Moves page up.
Ctrl-→	Moves word left.
Ctrl-S	Moves cursor left.
Ctrl-T	Deletes word right.
Ctrl-W	Deletes word left
Ctrl-X	Moves cursor down one line.
Ctrl-Y	Deletes line.
Del	Deletes character under cursor.
↓	Moves cursor down one line.
End	Moves to end of a line.
Esc	Quits edit.
F1	Selects help.
F10	Quits edit.
F2	Saves.
F7	Searches.
Home	Moves to beginning of a line.
←	Moves cursor left.
PgDn	Moves page down.
PgUp	Moves page up.
→	Moves cursor right.
Shift-F10	Saves and quits.
Shift-F2	Asks for name to save as.
Shift-F7	Continues search.
↑	Moves cursor up one line.

Using a Mouse

Although you do not need a mouse to use Norton
Commander, complete mouse support is available.
Using a mouse with Norton Commander makes using
the program easier.

When using a mouse in The Norton Commander, you
can use both mouse buttons.

Procedures

To move the cursor, single-click the left mouse button.

To scroll up or down, single-click the left mouse button
and drag to the top or bottom border.

To move a directory, point and shoot a file or launch an
application, double-click the left mouse button.

To select or unselect a file, single-click the right mouse
button.

To highlight and select files, single-click the right mouse
button on a file name and drag to additional files.

Dialog boxes

Single-click either mouse button on a dialog box button
to execute that action.

Single-click the right mouse button outside of a dialog
box to accept the highlighted action.

Menus

Single-click either button on the top line of the screen to
display the menu bar.

Single-click either button on a menu item to execute the
item.

Hold down the Shift key and single-click either button
on a menu item to execute the shifted version.

General

Press and release both mouse buttons simultaneously to
cancel a command or dismiss a dialog box (same as
pressing the Esc key).

Auto Menus

NC

Purpose

Appears with the main or local menu automatically. When turned on, Auto menus display the menu as soon as The Norton Commander is started and after the execution of each command.

Procedures

To use an Auto menu, press F9, and select Options, Auto menus, and press Enter.

To turn off the Auto menu option, press F9, and select Options, Auto menus, and press Enter.

Notes

Auto menu displays a menu until you press Esc.

You can use Auto menus to store a series of sequences you prefer when you start The Norton Commander. Simply include those commands in a user menu. Make sure that the menu is included in the directory and select Auto menus. This option is helpful if you do most of your work in The Norton Commander by using the menus, as you do not have to keep using F2.

Brief

NC

Purpose

Sets panel display to a brief directory listing.

Procedures

To display the Left panel in Brief:

1. Press F9.

2. Select Left and Brief.

To display the Right panel in Brief:

1. Press F9.

2. Select Right and Brief.

Notes

Subdirectories are displayed in uppercase letters. Files are displayed in lowercase letters. All files and directories are displayed within three columns in Brief.

You can use any of these keys when you select Brief:

-	Unselects a group of files.
+	Selects a group of files.
Alt-key	Speeds search.
Ctrl-\	Changes to the root directory ("CD\").
Ctrl-Enter	Looks for next match.
Ctrl-PgUp	Changes to the parent directory ("CD..").
Enter	Points and shoots.
Ins	Selects or unselects file under cursor.

Clock

NC

Purpose

Displays a clock in the upper-right corner of the screen.

Procedures

To display the clock:

1. Press F9.

2. Select Options, cLock, and press Enter.

To no longer display the clock:

1. Press F9.

2. Select Options, cLock, and press Enter.

Color

NC

Purpose

Enables you to set the display of your computer to color, black and white, or a special laptop display.

Procedures

1. Press F9.

2. Select Options, Color.

   A dialog box appears.

3. Select Black and White, Color, or Laptop.

Commands

NC

Purpose

Controls the commands available within The Norton Commander. Within this menu, the following options are available:

> NCD Tree
> Find File
> History
> EGA Lines
> Swap Panels
> Panels On/off
> Compare Directories
> Menu File Edit
> EXtension File Edit

Each option is fully explained in its own section within this Quick Reference.

Procedure

To display the Commands menu, press **F9** and select Commands.

Compare Directories

NC

Purpose

Compares the two directories displayed in the left and right panel. Files found in one directory but not the other directory are marked. Files created or edited more recently than the other also are marked by Compare Directories.

Procedures

1. Press **F9**.

2. Select Command, Compare Directories.

3. If both directories are exactly the same, The Norton Commander displays a message advising you that the directories are identical. Then press **Enter**.

Notes

You cannot use this command unless both panels are visible. If you attempt to use this command when both panels are not visible, an alert box advises you of the problem.

Copy

NC

Purpose

Copies all marked files to a specified location.

Procedures

1. Select the file or files to be copied.

2. Press F9.

3. Select Files and Rename/Move and press Enter.

   or

   Press F6.

4. Type the destination and press Enter.

Notes

If you try to copy more files than one floppy disk can hold, The Norton Commander stops so that you can place another disk in the drive.

If a file with the same name exits in the destination directory, an alert box appears. You then can skip or overwrite the existing file. You also can choose to overwrite all existing files.

Press Shift-F5 to display a different Copy dialog box. This box contains an area where you type the file or files to be copied, plus an area where you can specify the target or destination of the files.

Press Ctrl-Break to interrupt Copy.

Delete

NC

Purpose

Deletes a single file, a group of files, or an empty directory.

Procedures

1. Use the cursor-movement keys to highlight the file you want deleted.

2. Press F9.

3. Select Files, Delete, and then press Enter.

    or

    Press F8.

4. Press Enter to confirm the deletion.

    If a group of files are marked, all the files are deleted when Delete is accessed. Before any files are deleted with Delete, a dialog box appears, and you must confirm the deletion.

5. Select Delete to remove the displayed file, or press Esc or C to prevent the file or directory from being deleted.

Notes

Before you can delete a directory, it must be empty.

Press Shift-F8 to display a dialog box where you can type the name of a file or group of files to delete. If you use the Shift-F8 option, the files are deleted when you press Enter. You do not have to confirm the deletion.

Press Ctrl-Break to cancel the deletion of multiple files.

Directory Sort Options

NC

Purpose

Sorts the order of displayed files within the left or right panel. The files can be sorted by Name, Extension, Time, Size, or Unsorted.

Procedures

To sort files by name:

To sort files by name in the left panel, do the following:

1. Press F9.

2. Select the Left panel.

3. Select Name.

To sort files by extension:

To sort files by extension in the left panel, do the following:

1. Press F9.

2. Select the Left panel.

3. Select eXtenstion.

To sort files by time:

To sort files by time in the left panel, do the following:

1. Press F9.

2. Select the Left panel.

3. Select Time.

To sort files by size:

To sort files by size in the left panel, do the following:

1. Press F9.

2. Select the Left panel.

3. Select Size.

To display unsorted files:

To display unsorted files in the left panel, do the following:

1. Press F9.

2. Select the Left panel.

3. Select Unsorted.

Drive

NC

Purpose

Enables you to select the drive you want displayed in either the Left or Right panel.

Procedures

To select drives in the Right panel:

1. Press **F9**.

2. Select the **R**ight panel.

3. Select **D**rive and press the letter of the drive you want.

   or

   Press **Alt-F2** and then press the drive letter.

To select drives in the Left panel:

1. Press **F9**.

2. Select the **L**eft panel.

3. Select **D**rive and then press the letter of the drive you want.

   or

   Press **Alt-F1** and then press the drive letter.

Note

If you specify a drive that does not contain a disk, an alert box appears to advise you of the problem.

═│ **Edit** │══════════════════════════════

NC

Purpose

Loads the highlighted or selected file into The Norton Commander's editor.

Procedures

1. Press **F9**.

2. Select **F**iles, **E**dit.

   or

   Press **F4** and press **Enter**.

Notes

You can edit files no larger than about 30K in The Norton Commander editor.

Press Shift-F4 to display a dialog box that enables you to edit a file other than the one highlighted.

Press Ctrl-Q to insert a control character. For example, if you need to insert Ctrl-A in your text, press Ctrl-Q, then Ctrl-A.

You can use any of the following keys when using The Norton Commander editor:

F1 (Help) displays help information.

F2 (Save) saves any changes made with the editor to the disk.

Shift-F2 (Save As) saves the file under a different name.

F7 (Search) searches for a text string. Type the text to be searched in the dialog box and press Enter. If the string is not located, a message appears.

Shift-F7 (Repeats Search Edit) remembers the string entered. You can search for the next occurrence without retyping Shift-F7.

F10 (Quit) exits the Editor and returns you to The Norton Commander screen. If you attempt to quit without saving the changes, an alert box appears.

Shift-F10 (Save & Quit) saves your edited changes and leaves the Editor, returning you to The Norton Commander screen.

These key commands are available when you use Edit:

Backspace	Deletes character left.
Ctrl-A	Moves word left.
Ctrl-Backspace	Deletes word left.
Ctrl-C	Moves page down.

Ctrl-D	Moves cursor right.
Ctrl-E	Moves cursor up one line.
Ctrl-End	Moves to end of a file.
Ctrl-F	Moves word right.
Ctrl-G	Deletes character under cursor.
Ctrl-Home	Moves to start of a file.
Ctrl-K	Deletes to end of line.
Ctrl-←	Moves word right.
Ctrl-PgDn	Moves to end of a file.
Ctrl-PgUp	Moves to start of a file.
Ctrl-Q	Quotes next character.
Ctrl-R	Moves page up.
Ctrl-→	Moves word left.
Ctrl-S	Moves cursor left.
Ctrl-T	Deletes word right.
Ctrl-W	Deletes word left.
Ctrl-X	Moves cursor down one line.
Ctrl-Y	Deletes line.
Del	Deletes character under cursor.
↓	Moves cursor down one line.
End	Moves to end of a line.
Esc	Quits edit.
F1	Selects help.
F10	Quits edit.
F2	Saves.

F7	Searches.
Home	Moves to beginning of a line.
←	Moves cursor left.
PgDn	Moves page down.
PgUp	Moves page up.
→	Moves cursor right.
Shift-F10	Saves and quits.
Shift-F2	Asks for name to save as.
Shift-F7	Continues search.
↑	Moves cursor up one line.

Editor

NC

Purpose

Specifies (and enables you to choose) which text editor you want to use when you call the Edit command in the Files menu.

Procedures

1. Press F9.

2. Select Options, Editor.

3. Select External.

4. Type FILENAME and press Enter.

If the path to the external editor is not set in the AUTOEXEC.BAT file, you can specify the path in the Editor to Use window as C:\WP50\WP, for example.

Notes

When the Editor option is selected, you can specify which editor you want to use in a dialog box that

appears on your screen. If you choose to specify another
editor, type the name of the external editor in the Edit
dialog box. You must also specify how much of the file
name to use when The Norton Commander loads the
programs.

Type ! to indicate only the file name. Type !.! to indicate
the file name and the extension. Then press **Enter**.

EGA Lines

NC

Purpose

Changes the computer screen display from 25 to 43 lines
(if EGA) or between 25 and 50 lines, (if VGA). By
increasing the number of lines, you can see more files at
a time and more DOS output. Of course, the text is
smaller and harder to read.

Procedures

1. Press **F9**.

2. Select Commands, EGA Lines.

   or

   Press **Alt-F9** and press **Enter**.

Extension, Directory Sort

NC

Purpose

Sorts files in left or right panel by extension.

Procedures

To sort files in the left panel by extension:

1. Press **F9**.

2. Select Left, eXtension.

To sort files in the right panel by extension:
1. Press F9.
2. Select Right, eXtension.

Extension, File Edit

NC

Purpose

Enables you to modify NC.EXT files. Use in The Norton Commander to define which application program to associate with each extension, enabling you to load files with a single keystroke.

Procedures

1. Press F9.
2. Select Commands eXtension.

Notes

When the Extension File edit screen appears, a help panel at the bottom of the screen shows you how extension files are formatted.

Each line in the NC.EXT file associates one extension with a single application, and tells The Norton Commander what to place on the DOS command line when Enter is pressed or when the file name is double-clicked with a mouse). For example, the line

wp: /C WP !.!

tells The Norton Commander to load any files with the extension .WP into the application WP (presumed to be WordPerfect) if Enter is pressed with the highlight over the file name.

Make sure that the path is properly set in your AUTOEXEC.BAT file so that DOS can find your applications. Or, you can include an entire path by setting the line as

wp: C:\WP50\WP.EXE !.!

The !.! tells The Norton Commander to include the file name and extension on the command line. You can use these NC.EXT arguments:

!.!	Insert the file and its extension.
!	Insert on the file name and omit the extension.
!:	Insert the current drive letter followed by a colon.
!\	Insert the path name.
!!	Insert single exclamation point.

Files Menu

NC

Purpose

Controls the way the files within The Norton Commander are displayed. Within this menu, the following options are available:

Help (F1)
User menu (F2)
View (F3)
Edit (F4)
Copy (F5)
Rename/Move (F6)
Make Directory (F7)
Delete (F8)
Quit (F10)

Each option is fully explained in its own section within this Quick Reference.

Procedures

1. Press F9.

2. Select Files.

Find File

NC

Purpose

Enables you to search the entire current disk for a specific file or group of files. You can use the DOS wild cards * and ? as part of your search criteria.

Procedures

To search for a particular file:

To search the current drive for the file REPORT.JAN, do the following:

1. Press F9.

2. Select Commands, Find File.

   or

   Press Alt-F7.

3. Type REPORT.JAN and press Enter.

To search for a file with a particular extension:

To search the current drive for all files with the .LTR extension, do the following:

1. Press F9.

2. Select Commands, Find File.

   or

   Press Alt-F7.

2. Type *.LTR and press Enter.

Notes

After selecting Find File, a panel is displayed. Type the name of the file or files you want to locate and press Enter to begin the search. Each file that matches the search specification appears in the panel.

While searching, you can scroll back through the list to see the files that are displayed.

Move the file selection bar to the right file and press **Enter** to switch to the file's directory and highlight the found file. Or, you can move the highlight to the New Search button and press **Enter** to start a new search. You also can move the highlight to the Quit FF button and press **Enter**.

Pressing **Esc** dismisses the Find File panel.

Full

NC

Purpose

Sets the panel display to a full directory listing, displaying information in four columns. The information displayed includes the file or directory name, the size of the file or directory, the date and time of the last modification of the directory or file.

Procedures

To display full file and directory information in the Left File panel:

1. Press **F9**.

2. Select **L**eft, **F**ull.

To display full file and directory information in the Right File panel:

1. Press **F9**.

2. Select **R**ight, **F**ull.

Notes

You can use any of these keys when you select Brief:

-	Unselect a group of files.
+	Select a group of files.
Alt-key	Speed Search.

Ctrl-\	Change to the root directory ("CD\").
Ctrl-Enter	Look for next match.
Ctrl-PgUp	Change to the parent directory ("CD..").
Enter	Point and shoot.
Ins	Select, unselect file under cursor.

Full Screen

NC

Purpose

Controls the size of both panels. With the option turned on, both panels use most of the computer screen. With the option turned off, the left and right panels are displayed about one-half the size, leaving room to see more of your screen and previous DOS commands.

Procedures

1. Press F9.

2. Select Options, Full Screen.

Help

NC

Purpose

Presents keyboard commands available in The Norton Commander. Once the Help screen is displayed, press any key to dismiss the Help screen.

Procedures

1. Press F9.

2. Select Files, Help.

or

Press F1.

History

Purpose

Presents a list of the last 15 DOS commands used.

Procedures

To use History from the keyboard:

1. Press F9.

2. Select Commands, History.

   or

   Press Alt-F8.

2. Use the cursor-movement keys to scroll though the list of previous DOS commands.

3. Move the highlight bar to the command and press Enter.

To use History with a mouse:

1. Move the mouse cursor to the desired command, and click the left mouse button once to highlight the command.

2. Click the right mouse button once to execute the command. Or, double-click the left mouse button to select and execute the command.

Notes

The following keyboard commands work like History. They include:

Ctrl-E   Places the last DOS command
                          on the command line

Ctrl-X   Places the next DOS command
                          on the command line (should
                          you skip over it with too many
                          Ctrl-E commands)

Ctrl-Enter   If characters are on the DOS
                          command line, Ctrl-Enter
                          places the last command
                          beginning with those letters on
                          the command line.

Info

NC

Purpose

Sets the panel to display information about the directory.

Procedures

To display Info in the Left panel:
1. Press F9.

2. Select Left, Info.

To display Info in the Right panel:
1. Press F9.

2. Select Right, Info.

Notes

The Info panel is displayed in three sections. The top
section displays copyright information about The Norton
Commander. The middle section displays information
about the total amount of system memory that is
available, the amount of system memory that is free, the
total capacity of the current drive, and the total amount
of space used on the current drive. The bottom area
contains any information about the current directory
stored in the file DIRINFO. You can use F4 to edit any
information displayed in the bottom section of the Info
panel.

Use **Ctrl-L** to change an active panel to an Info panel, or to change an Info Panel to a directory panel.

Ins Moves Down

NC

Purpose

Controls the file selection bar when a file is marked with the Insert key.

Procedures

1. Press **F9**.

2. Select **O**ptions, **I**ns Moves Down.

Note

When Ins Moves Down is unchecked or turned off, the file selection bar remains stationary and does not move when Ins is pressed to mark a file.

Key Bar

Purpose

Displays or removes the Function Key Bar at the bottom of the computer screen.

Procedures

1. Press **F9**.

2. Select **O**ptions, **K**ey bar.

   or

   Press **Ctrl-B**.

Left

NC

Purpose

Controls the Left Panel. Within this menu, the following options are available:

Brief
Full
Info
Tree
On/Off (Ctrl-F1)
Name
EXtension
TiMe
Size
Unsorted
Re-read
Drive (Alt-F1)

The commands and display options available within this menu are grouped into three sets. These commands and options determine whether the Left Panel is displayed, and if so, how the information in it appears.

The first set of options, Brief, Full, Info, Tree, and On/Off, control the type of panel displayed on the left side of your screen. You can select only one of these options at a time.

The second set of options, Name, Extension, Time, Size, and Unsorted, control the order in which the files and directories are displayed within the Left Panel.

The third set of options within the Left menu enables you to read directories and change drives.

Each option is fully explained in its own section within this Quick Reference.

Procedures

1. Press F9.

2. Select Left.

Make Directory

NC

Purpose

Creates new directories on your drive. This command is
similar to the DOS MD or MKDIR command.

Procedures

1. Press F9.

2. Select Files, Make Directory.

   or

   Press F7 and then press Enter.

   A Make Directory dialog box appears.

3. Type the name of the new directory (eight or less
   characters long) in the Make Directory dialog box,
   then press Enter.

Menu File Edit

NC

Purpose

Enables you to modify any NC.MNU file. You also can
use to create your own menus.

Procedures

1. Press F9.

2. Select Commands, Menu File Edit.

   A dialog box asks you to specify which user menu
   you want to edit. You can edit the main menu or
   a local menu. If no local menu exists, you can
   create one.

3. Specify the menu you want to edit.

The Menu File Edit screen appears. At the bottom of the screen is a help panel showing you how menu files are formatted.

4. Type or edit the menu text.

The first line contains an option key to press to access the item, followed by a colon, and the name to appear in the menu itself. For example, W:WordPerfect 5.0 on the first line of a menu puts the line WordPerfect 5.0 in the user menu. You can access WordPerfect by typing W. To omit the hotkey, leave out the colon and type the entire name flush left.

All subsequent lines within a single menu item must be valid DOS commands and must be indented. Separate items by a blank line.

Mini Status

NC

Purpose

Controls the status line at the bottom of the Left or Right panel. The status line displays the name, size, or subdirectories, and the date and time of the last modification of the file highlighted with the file selection bar.

Procedures

1. Press F9.

2. Select Options, Mini Status.

Notes

With the Mini status unchecked or turned off, the status line does not appear. Within the two additional lines, The Norton Commander displays the file and directory names.

Name, Directory Sort

NC

Purpose

Sorts files in Left or Right panel by name.

Procedures

To sort files in the Left panel by name:

1. Press F9.

2. Select Left, Name.

To sort files in the Right panel by name:

1. Press F9.

2. Select Right, Name.

NCD Tree

NC

Purpose

Displays a graphical representation of the path structure of your disk in a pop-up window.

Procedures

To display the NCD tree:

1. Press F9,

2. Select Commands, NCD Tree.

   or

   Press Alt-F10, and then press Enter.

To exit the NCD tree:

Press F10.

or

Press Esc.

To rescan the current disk:
Press F2 and press Enter.

To select a directory:
1. Move the highlight to the desired directory.

2. Press Enter.

To rename a directory:
1. Highlight the desired directory.

2. Press F6.

3. Type the new name of the directory.

4. Press Enter.

To make a directory:
1. Move the highlight to the directory where the subdirectory is to be added.

2. Press F7.

3. Type the name of the new directory.

4. Press Enter.

To delete a directory:
1. Move the highlight to the desired directory.

2. Press F8.

Notes

The NCD Tree command displays a directory tree similar to the one shown when using the Tree command in the Left or Right menu.

You can use the cursor-movement keys to move the highlight bar from one directory to another. If you press Enter, the NCD tree disappears from the screen, and the highlighted directory becomes the current directory. This command is similar to the DOS CD or CHDIR commands.

You can use the speed search function located at the bottom of the NCD tree window. Simply type the name of the directory. As you type, the text appears in the panel at the bottom of your screen. The highlight also moves to the first directory that matches the text entered

so far. If you type the letter **W**, the highlight moves to
the first directory that begins with a "W". If there is no
directory that begins with a "W", then the highlight does
not move.

You can continue to type to narrow the search. Press
Ctrl+Enter to search for the next potential match.

You can use any of these function keys while using the
NCD tree:

> **F2** rescans the current disk and then rebuilds the
> TREEINFO.NCD file. Use this command if
> directories were added or deleted outside The
> Norton Commander.

> **F6** renames a selected or highlighted directory. Type
> the new name of the directory, and press **Enter**.

> **F7** creates or makes a new directory. The new
> directory appears as a subdirectory of the directory
> under the highlight. Enter the new name of the
> directory, and press **Enter**.

> **F8** deletes the highlighted or selected directory. A
> directory must be empty before it can be deleted.

> **F10** exits the NCD tree display and returns you to
> The Norton Commander screen. You can also press
> **Esc** to exit the NCD tree display.

On/Off

NC

Purpose

Turns the Left and Right panels on and off.

Procedures

To turn off the Left panel:

1. Press **F9**.

   2. Select Left, On/Off.

      or

      Press Ctrl-F1.

To turn off the Right panel:
   1. Press F9.

   2. Select Right, On/Off.

      or

      Press Ctrl-F2.

To turn on the Left panel:
   1. Press F9.

   2. Select Left, On/Off.

      or

      Press Ctrl-F1.

To turn on the Right panel:
   1. Press F9.

   2. Select Right, On/Off.

      or

      Press Ctrl-F2.

To turn off the inactive panel:
   Press Ctrl-P.

To turn off or on both panels:
   Press Ctrl-O.

Options

NC

Purpose

   Controls the options available within The Norton
   Commander. The following options are available:

Color
Auto menus
Path Prompt
Key Bar (Ctrl-B)
Full Screen
Mini Status
Ins Moves down
CLock
Editor
Save Setup (Shift-F9)

Each option is fully explained in its own section within this Quick Reference.

Procedures

   1. Press F9.

   2. Select Options.

Panels On/Off

NC

Purpose

   Exchanges the panels, swapping what is displayed on the Left panel into the Right panel.

Procedures

   1. Press F9.

   2. Select Commands, Swap Panels.

     or

     Press Ctrl-U.

=Path Prompt

NC

Purpose

Controls the DOS command line prompt. For example, with the Path Prompt checked or turned on, the DOS command line prompt shows the drive letter and the current path name, such as

```
C:\LOTUS\REPORTS>
```

With the option unchecked or turned off, the DOS command line prompt only shows the current drive letter

```
C>
```

Procedures

1. Type F9.

2. Select Options, Path Prompt.

=Quit

NC

Purpose

Enables you to leave or exit The Norton Commander.

Procedures

1. Press F9.

2. Select Files, Quit.

   or

   Press F10, and press Enter.

Rename/Move

Purpose

Renames a file or group of files in a directory. You also can move files from one directory to another.

Procedures

1. Select the file or files to be moved or renamed.

2. Press F9.

3. Select Files, Rename/Move.

   or

   Press F6.

4. Type the destination (path name or directory) where the marked file or files are to be moved and press Enter.

Notes

If you try to move more files onto a floppy disk than it can hold, The Norton Commander stops so that you can place another disk in the drive, and then continues.

Press Shift-F6 to see a different Rename/Move dialog box. This box contains an area where you type the file or files to be moved or renamed, plus an area where you can specify the target or destination of the files.

Press Ctrl-Break to interrupt Rename/Move.

Re-read

Purpose

Rereads the displayed directory in the Left or Right panel, and then updates the display within the panel.

Procedures

To re-read the Left panel:

1. Press F9.

2. Select **L**eft, **R**e-read.

To re-read the Right panel:

1. Press F9.

2. Select **R**ight, **R**e-read.

To re-read the active panel:

Press Ctrl-R.

Notes

Usually, the display within the panel is updated automatically. However, if you change diskettes, you may need to use this command. Re-read is used to update the panel, when needed.

Right

NC

Purpose

Controls the Right Panel. Within this menu, the following options are available:

Brief
Full
Info
Tree
On/Off (Ctrl—F1)
Name
E**X**tension
Ti**M**e
Size
Unsorted
Re-read
Drive (Alt-F1)

The commands and display options available within this menu are grouped into three sets. These commands and options determine whether the Right Panel is displayed, and if so, how the information in it is displayed.

The first set of options, Brief, Full, Info, Tree, and On/Off, control the type of panel displayed on the fight side of your screen. You can select only one of these options at a time. A check mark appears next to the current selection.

The second set of options, Name, Extension, Time, Size, and Unsorted, controls the order in which the files and directories are displayed within the Right Panel.

The third set of options within the Right menu enables you to reread directories and change drives.

Each option is fully explained in its own section within this Quick Reference.

Procedures

1. Press F9.

2. Select R ight.

Save Setup

NC

Purpose

Enables you to save the current settings.

Procedures

1. Press F9.

2. Select O ptions, S ave Setup.

   or

   Press Shift-F9 and press Enter.

3. Select S ave and press Enter, or select C ancel.

Notes

> When you save the current settings with Save Setup, The Norton Commander remembers all the options you selected in the various menus. The next time you run The Norton Commander, all the chosen options are displayed. The settings are saved in a file called NC.INI.

Size, Directory Sort

NC

Purpose

> Sorts files in the Left or Right panel by size.

Procedures

> ***To sort files in the Left panel by size:***
>
> 1. Press F9 .
>
> 2. Select L eft, S ize.
>
> ***To sort files in the Right panel by size:***
>
> 1. Press F9 .
>
> 2. Select R ight, S ize.

Swap Panels

NC

Purpose

> Exchanges the Left and Right panels, moving them to the other position.

Procedures

> 1. Press F9 .

2. Select Commands, Swap Panels.

or

Press Ctrl-U.

Notes

If only one panel is displayed, the Swap Panel command moves the single panel to the other side. If both panels are displayed, they are swapped between the panels.

Time, Directory Sort

NC

Purpose

Sorts files in the Left or Right panel by time.

Procedures

To sort files in the Left panel by time:
1. Press F9.
2. Select Left, TiMe.

To sort files in the Right panel by time:
1. Press F9.
2. Select Right, TiMe.

Tree

NC

Purpose

Sets the Left or Right panel to display a graphical directory tree of the current drive.

Procedures

To display a tree in the Left panel:
1. Press F9.

2. Select Left, Tree.

To display a tree in the Right panel:
1. Press F9.

2. Select Right, Tree.

Note

You can scroll through the directories in the tree by pressing the cursor-movement keys. To select a directory, press Enter.

Unsorted, Directory

NC

Purpose

Displays files in the Left or Right panel in unsorted order.

Procedures

To display files in the Left panel unsorted:
1. Press F9.

2. Select Left, Unsorted.

To display files in the Right panel unsorted:
1. Press F9.

2. Select Right, Unsorted.

User Menu

NC

Purpose

Causes The Norton Commander to display a user menu. Different applications can be accessed from this menu.

Procedures

1. Press F9.

2. Select Files, User Menu.

or

Press F2 and press Enter.

Notes

The options available from the User menu are stored in a file called NC.MNU, which is created and edited with the Menu file edit option, available in the Commands menu.

You can create a different user menu in each directory, if you want. By doing so, you can customize each different menu to handle the particular files stored in your various directories.

Each user-defined command in a user menu must contain one or more DOS commands. A user menu is much like a DOS batch file.

You can issue a particular command within a user menu by moving the highlight, or by selecting the appropriate key shown next to the option within the menu. You can also double-click your mouse on any of the options displayed within the menu.

View

NC

Purpose

Displays a file. Similar to the DOS TYPE command, except that it offers many additional features. You can scroll through a selected file, and you can search for a particular character string within the file. If the file you are viewing is a dBASE II, III, or IV file, a Lotus 1-2-3, or a Symphony file, you can see the file contents in either spreadsheet or data format.

Procedures

1. Move the highlight to the file to be viewed.

2. Press F9.

3. Select Files, View.

or

Press F3 and then press Enter.

___

Notes

Files with the extensions of .WKS or .WK1 (Lotus 1-2-3) or .WRK and .WRL (Lotus Symphony) are displayed in spreadsheet format. Files with the extension .DBF are shown in a database format. When displaying a dBASE II, III, or IV file, a Lotus 1- 2-3, or a Symphony file, you can override the special view feature and see the file in regular text format by pressing Alt-F3

First select a file to be viewed by moving the highlight. Or, another file can be viewed by pressing Shift-F3 A dialog box appears, and you can type the name of the file to view. Press Enter to begin viewing the file.

View displays a panel over the entire screen. At the top of the View panel, the name of the file being viewed and its path is displayed. You can use the cursor-movement keys, PgUp, PgDn, Home, or End to scroll through the file's contents.

You can use any of these function keys while using the NCD tree:

F7 enables you to search for a text string. After pressing F7, a dialog box appears. Type the text to be searched, and press Enter. You can type the string in upper- or lowercase. If the string is not located, a message appears advising you so.

Shift-F7 remembers the string entered, and if you want, you can search for the next occurrence without retyping it by simply pressing Shift-F7.

F10 exits the View display and returns you to The Norton Commander screen. You can also press Esc to exit the View display. Text cannot be changed when using View.

When you view a database file, the view screen includes the record number of the database currently being displayed. One record is shown at a time, with the contents of one filed per line. Use the up- or down-arrow to see additional fields that cannot be seen on the screen.

F1 displays additional information about the data base file being viewed. Press any key to dismiss the information box displayed with this command.

F2 displays a window that shows the name of each field, the field type, and the field size. Press Esc to dismiss the fields information box.

F5 enables you to move rapidly through the database file. F5 displays a small dialog box where you type the record number you wish to view. Press Enter, and Database View displays the selected record. If you type in a number larger than the actual database, you move to the bottom of the data base.

F7 enables you to search for a text string in Database view. After pressing F7, a dialog box appears. Type the text to be searched, and press Enter to begin the search process. When the text is located in a record, the record is displayed. If the string is not located in any of the records, a message appears advising you so. A long search can be interrupted by pressing Ctrl-Break.

Shift-F7 remembers the string entered, and if desired, you can search for the next occurrence without retyping by pressing Shift-F7.

F10 exits the dBASE View, and returns to The Norton Commander screen.

dBASE View keys

You can use any of these keys when viewing a database file:

-	Moves to previous record.
+	Moves to next record.
Ctrl-Break	Stops a long search.

Ctrl-E	Scrolls back one field.
Ctrl-End	Moves to last record.
Ctrl-Home	Moves to first record.
Ctrl-PgDn	Moves to last record.
Ctrl-PgUp	Moves to first record.
Ctrl-R	Pages up previous record.
Esc	Quits dBASE view.
F1	Provides general information.
F10	Quits dBASE view.
F2	Provides field information.
F5	Goes to a record.
F7	Searches.
PgUp	Pages up previous record.
Shift-F7	Continues search.
Up Arrow	Scrolls back one field.

When viewing a Lotus 1-2-3 or Symphony worksheet file, the View screen includes the cell address. A cell pointer is also displayed, and can be used for viewing the contents of different cells within the spreadsheet.

To change from the Lotus view to a regular text view, press Alt-F3.

Press F10 or Esc to exit Lotus view.

LotusView keys

You can use any of these keys when viewing a Lotus file:

Ctrl-C	Moves page down.
Ctrl-D	Moves cell right.
Ctrl-E	Moves cell up.
Ctrl-←	Scrolls left one page.
Ctrl-R	Moves page up.

Ctrl-→	Scrolls right one. Page.
Ctrl-S	Moves cell left.
Ctrl-Z	Moves cell down.
↓	Moves cell down.
End	Moves to last active cell.
Esc	Quits Lotus view.
F10	Quits Lotus view.
Home	Moves to top, left cell (A1).
←	Moves cell left.
PgDn	Moves page down.
PgUp	Moves page up.
→	Moves cell right.
Shift-Tab	Scrolls left one page.
Tab	Scrolls right one page.
↑	Moves cell up.

Index